C000132880

Witness

images of the decade

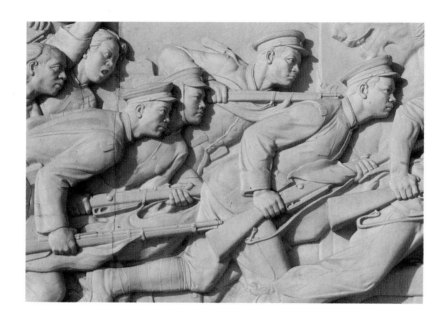

Julian Calder

Carving in Tiananmen Square
— monument to the People's heroes.

Beijing, China November 1987

Witness

images of the decade

Nikon

VIRGIN
optomen

▨ Sports Editions Ltd

Managing Director	Richard Dewing
Art Director/Picture Editor	Mary Hamlyn
Senior Designer	Rob Kelland
Designers	Sandra Cowell
	Alex Evans
Consultant Editor	Peter Hayter
Editor	Leslie Smillie
Editorial Assistant	Joanna Mawson

Copyright © Sports Editions Ltd/Nikon UK Ltd 1990

All rights reserved. No part of this publication may be reproduced, stored in a retrieval system, or transmitted in any form or by any means, electronic, mechanical, photocopying, recording or otherwise without prior permission of the copyright holders.

First published in 1990 by
Virgin Optomen
26 Grand Union Centre
338 Ladbroke Grove
London W10 5AH

This book is sold subject to the condition that it shall not, by way of trade or otherwise, be lent, re-sold, hired or otherwise circulated without prior consent in any form of binding or cover other than that in which it is published and without a similar condition including this condition being imposed upon the subsequent purchaser.

ISBN 1-85 227-342-9

Produced, edited and designed by
Sports Editions Ltd
3 Greenlea Park
Prince George's Road
London SW19 2JD

Typeset in Bauer Bodoni and Walbaum by Sports Editions. Colour origination by Sonic Plates, London EC1. Black and white reproduction, printing and binding by BAS, Stockbridge, Hampshire. Printed on MultiArt Silk which has the seal of approval of the Swedish Enviromental Resarch Group; produced from renewable wood supplies, it uses no chlorine gas during the bleaching process.

Acknowledgements

I would like to thank: Harry Collins at Nikon UK Ltd for inviting me to edit and produce his idea; Richard Dewing and Steve Powell for providing the initial impetus when I was faced with the real enormity of this project; the publishers who have been a steady source of support and encouragement; the whole team at Sports Editions for their understanding and extreme diligence during the production of *Witness*; Colin Jacobson for his advice right at the start of the project; and my special thanks go to the photographers who were invariably generous with their time, their information and their encouragement; and whose wonderful courage, insight and vision made it possible to create *Witness*.

Mary Hamlyn
Editorial Director

Contents

FOREWORD
PAGE 7
Harry Collins of Nikon UK Ltd

THE CONTRIBUTORS
PAGE 8
Biographies of the contributors

SCENES FROM EVERYDAY LIFE
PAGE 12
Essay by Trevor McDonald

SPORTING LIFE
PAGE 118
Essay by Ian Wooldridge

UNIVERSAL MATTERS
PAGE 84
Essay by Marcus Binney

STARS OF STAGE AND SCREEN
PAGE 140
Essay by John Kobal

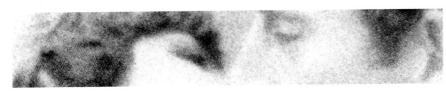

RULING CLASS
PAGE 102
Essay by Unity Hall

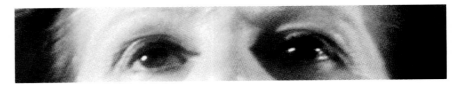

GOVERNING BODIES
PAGE 162
Essay by Simon Hoggart

Roger Hutchings

New Prague Spring — young soldiers celebrate with demonstrators after the resignation of the Communist government in the face of popular protest.

Wenceslas Square, Prague, Czechoslovakia 29th November 1989

Foreword

Witness — images of the decade started off very modestly and almost of its own volition grew into something which I feel is tremendously exciting, and a privilege for our company to sponsor.

In looking for ideas as to how we could celebrate our tenth anniversary, I was convinced that it should recognise the talents, the skills, the dedication and the sheer hard work of photographers who use our equipment and had in fact ensured our success throughout our first ten years.

When I first mentioned the idea of a book to photographers I was amazed by their enthusiasm and willingness to participate. As the project gathered momentum and more and more photographers offered their work for inclusion I became more excited but at the same time very humble that so many of my friends wished to help.

What really makes *Witness* come alive is the skill and artistry of the photographers; the instinct to choose just the right moment, quite often in extremely arduous conditions and at great personal risk. Throughout the book we have tried to use these images in a way that does not compromise the integrity of the picture or the photographer. I am also privileged to have some of the best writers represented here whose unique observations add to the book's flavour. Each of the photographers agreed to provide their work free and all profits from the book will be donated to Action Research For the Crippled Child, one of the best organised Children's Charities in the UK.

There are no adequate words to express my thanks to all those involved in this project. My one wish is that *Witness* enjoys the success it richly deserves — so that everyone can feel justly proud of their participation.

Harry Collins
Director and General Manager
Nikon UK Ltd

The contributors

MIKE ABRAHAMS
began his career in photography 15 years ago working for major newspapers and magazines. In 1981 he was a founding member of the Network Photographers Agency and in 1989 the book which he co-authored, *Still War* — based on the troubles in Northern Ireland — was published.

HEATHER ANGEL
originally trained as a zoologist. Her interest in photography developed while scuba diving and she began by taking pictures of marine life. She has been a freelance wildlife photographer and author for 17 years and manages her own photo library, examples from which are reproduced worldwide to illustrate books, magazines, posters, etc. The 39 books she has written and illustrated include: *The Natural History of Britain and Ireland* (co-author, 1981), *The Book of Close-up Photography* (1982), *Heather Angel's Countryside* (1984), *Nature in Focus* (1988), and *Landscape Photography* (1989). Her current projects include photographing Arctic wildlife and the use of photography to aid worldwide conservation.

H. J. P. 'DOUGLAS' ARNOLD
began experimenting with photography while at Wadham College, Oxford using very simple cameras. After graduating, he became a Russian specialist in the Intelligence Corps during his national service, before moving on to be Foreign News Editor and Soviet Affairs Correspondent for *The Financial Times*. He became increasingly involved in technological matters and from 1966 to 1974 was an assistant to the Managing Director of Kodak. He then formed Space Frontiers Limited, which he manages. He has written several books, including *Images from Space* and *Night Sky Photography*, and is a frequent contributor to spaceflight, astronomy and photography magazines. His TV appearances include *The Sky at Night* and he was a member of the studio team during BBC coverage of the later Apollo missions.

DAVID ASHDOWN
started in photography after leaving school, joining the Keystone Press as a motorcycle despatch rider. Two years later he worked as a dark room printer, before becoming a photographer covering news and sport in 1974. In 1978 he moved to the *Daily Star*, concentrating on sports photography. Among his many awards are Ilford Press Photographer of the Year (1977), runner-up in the British Press Awards (1979), Ilford Sports Picture of the Year (1985), Nikon Sports Picture of the Year (1987) and Sports Photographer of the Year (1987). Since 1986 he has been Chief Sports Photographer for *The Independent*.

MARCUS BINNEY O.B.E. F.S.A.
began as an architectural writer to *Country Life* and later served as editor. He is the founder and president of SAVE Britain's Heritage. and was awarded the O.B.E in 1983. He is one of Britain's leading conservation campaigners involved in many Trusts and campaigns: one of which is the Jersey Wildlife Preservation Trust; winner of the London Conservation medal 1985. He is involved in restoring Barlaston Hall, Staffordshire and writing a book on the architecture of seaside resorts.

MICHAEL BUSSELLE
took his first photographs at the age of eleven with a box camera, and his first professional experience was as a dye-transfer printer in a London colour laboratory. A spell as assistant to a leading advertising photographer was followed by a stint of freelance assignments, mainly travel, for a number of magazines and publishers. At 22 he started his own studio in London's West End, working on a number of projects but landscape and travel photography have remained his greatest pleasure. He has written over 20 books including the best-selling *Master Photography*, published by Mitchell Beazley in 1977, and *The Wine Lovers' Guide to France* published by Pavilion Books. He also writes and illustrates a number of features for a wide range of magazines including the *Telegraph Weekend* magazine, *Signature*. the *Sunday Express* magazine and *The Traveller*. His current projects include an illustrated large-format guide to French villages.

JULIAN CALDER
spent three years at Guildford Art School before working as a photographers assistant in London for another three years. His first assignment came in 1971 from *Nova* magazine to photograph the end of the 'Hippie Dream' in California. Throughout the last two decades he has worked mainly for British and American magazines shooting such events as the three Royal weddings, the Papal visit to the UK, the aftermath of the Falklands War and on patrol with Greenpeace. He was co-author of the million-selling *35mm Photographers Handbook*. Now much of his work takes him around the world shooting for corporate reports and magazine features.

NOBBY CLARK
started taking photographs for Michael Croft's National Youth Theatre in 1968. Since then he has worked for theatre companies, newspapers and in films.

MARTIN CLEAVER M.B.E.
started his career with the *Coventry Evening Telegraph*, first as an apprentice then later as a staff photographer, after gaining his NCTJ Diploma in Photography. He spent eight years with the Press Association before moving on to the *London Daily News* as a staff photographer. A period of freelance work for the *Telegraph* group and Associated Press led to his current position as a staff photographer for the Associated Press. His many assignments have included the Iranian Embassy siege in London, the Falklands War, the 1986 World Cup in Mexico, the Zeebrugge ferry disaster, the Prime Minister's tours of Poland and Africa, the Lockerbie bombing and the civil war in Lebanon. In 1983 he was made a MBE and in the same year he was named British Press Photographer of the Year, IIPP Photographer of the Year, Ilford Press/News Photographer of the Year and won the World Press Award for sport news.

RICHARD COOKE
did a Fine Arts course at Coventry College of Art and then became Art Buyer with an advertising agency in Birmingham, going on to become a photographer's agent. Six years later he gave this up to become an inventor but soon went back to photography which became a full-time job. While working on an RAF assignment he developed a new technique for taking pictures of fast jet aircraft coming head-on to the camera, using a wide-angle lens from a few feet away. The success of this venture led to his being commissioned to take pictures for RAF advertising. He has since developed similar techniques for other action subjects such as cars, helicopters and gliders.

STEPHEN DALTON
was first introduced to photography by his father, a keen naturalist and amateur bird photographer. His lasting interest in photography, however, did not develop until, in his early twenties, he gave up his dull office job to take a course in photography at the Regent Street Polytechnic and he is now recognised as one of the best nature photographers. He has published numerous books and his articles have appeared in a wide range of publications such as *National Geographic*, *Audubon Magazine* and many of the British colour supplements. His current interests include turning 45 acres of Sussex farmland into a wildlife sanctuary.

PATRICK EAGAR
began his career in photography immediately after graduating from university in 1965. His early work included various assignments for *Report*, including a four-month visit to Vietnam in 1966, and lots of coverage of West End theatre. His full-time move into the world of cricket photography came in 1970 and he covered his first Test match in 1972 — he has covered every Test match played in England since. Amongst his awards are winner in the colour section of the Rothman British Press Pictures of the Year in 1973; Highly Commended Portfolio, Sports Photographer of the Year in 1975, 1977, 1978 and 1983; and winner, B & W Portfolio (single sport), Sports Photographer of the Year 1988 and 1989. He has published several books, including *An Eye for Cricket* in 1979 (his first, with John Arlott) and *Tour of Tours*, his most recent with Alan Ross, and, since 1980, has also been involved in wine and vineyard photography.

SALLY FEAR
first became interested in photography when working in an advertising agency, going on to win many awards with her weekend photography efforts — one being the first Nikon scholarship in 1975 which enabled her to complete the project on 'London at the Weekend'. In 1978 this was a major exhibition at the National Theatre. She then became freelance and subsequently worked for many magazines, including the British Sunday supplements, *Life, Fortune, Newsweek* and *Time*. Her work has also featured in the books *A Day in the Life of Australia* and *A Day in the Life of London*. She is a founder Member of the agency Impact Photos, and was also the Editor and Managing Director. In 1988 she became the Deputy Director of The Photographer's Gallery in London.

JILL FURMANOVSKY
spent three years at the Central School of Art and Design, including a two-week block course in photography. She borrowed a camera to take a few photographs at a concert at the Rainbow Theatre where she was mistaken for a professional and was offered the unpaid post of Official Rainbow Photographer — she accepted and went on to become one of the best known photographers in the music business. *New Musical Express*, the style culture magazine *The Face* and *Smash Hits* magazine all commissioned her and in 1982 she moved into her own studio. If anything she now specialises in diversity: from the new Pretenders record sleeve to Ulster's Orange Order; from birth to businessmen. Her main project for 1990 is book of her own photography.

KENT GAVIN
began as an apprentice with the Keystone Press. After six years with them he joined the *Daily Mirror* in 1965, and he has since covered many major news situations — including the Vietnam war, Biafra, the Aden war and the Irish situation. His coverage of seal-clubbing in Canada resulted in the picture which was to become known worldwide and which eventually led to the seal hunt being abandoned. He has won over 80 major photographic awards, including British Press Photographer of the Year on

four occasions; Royal Photographer of the Year five times; Royal Photographer of the Decade; and World Press News and Feature Photograph of the Year. He has now photographed over 100 Royal tours.

MIKE GOLDWATER
has been taking pictures since the age of 12. He graduated from Sussex University in 1972, BSc in Physics, and was director of Half Moon Gallery in London 1974-1980. The results of a November 1979 trip to cover Khmer Rouge activities were published in *Now!* magazine. He co-founded Network Photographers Agency with seven others in January 1981 and between 1981 and 1990 he spent 18 months in Central America, covering the situation in Salvador, Nicaragua, Honduras and Guatemala. In 1984 he began a project on famine in the Sahel which resulted in the book *Fighting the Famine* published by Pluto Press in 1985. There was also a joint exhibition with Chris Steele-Perkins 'Famine in Africa' for the Side Gallery, which toured the UK. Since 1986 he has travelled widely covering assignments and stories for *The Observer, The Sunday Times, The Independent, The Daily Telegraph, Time* and *Stern* magazines. A picture from a set on AIDS in Uganda was highly commended in the 1987 World Press awards. He also photographed in Pakistan for the book *Indus Journey* to be published by Chatto and Windus in 1990.

TIM GRAHAM
left school and took a job as an assistant in a Fleet Street picture agency where he gradually took on various press photographic assignments. In 1968 he covered his first Royal tour to Austria, and his interest in photographing the Royal Family grew. Eventually, in 1978, after three years as a staff photographer with the *Daily Mail*, he became a freelance, specialising in Royalty. His photographs now appear regularly in all the major magazines throughout the world including the *Sunday Times Magazine, Vogue, Time, Newsweek, Paris Match* and have won him dozens of photographic awards. His work has also appeared in several books (*In Private, In Public — The Prince and Princess of Wales*

and *In Person* both became worldwide bestsellers) and each year a collection of his photographs are published in *The Royal Year*. Most of his time is now spent covering the many Royal trips.

ALAN GRISBROOK
attended evening classes in photography whilst working for the Electricity Board. His pictures of a famous stripper participating in a religous debate at Speakers Corner were published in *Titbits* magazine. He then started to freelance regularly for the *Evening News* and the *Standard* and now works mainly for the *Mirror Group Newspapers*. In March 1987 he won the monthly Nikon Press Award for his photograph of David Steel and Cleo Rocos which appears on page 163.

UNITY HALL
began her career in journalism as a tea-girl on a magazine. She has worked on newspapers and magazines since the 1940s and was the Woman's Editor for the *News of the World* for 18 years. She is now their agony aunt. Her most recent book on the Royals is *Royalty Revealed* with a new title due for publication in the autumn of 1990 — *Private Lives of Britain's Royal Women*. *House of Secrets* is her most recent novel and she is currently working on her next one.

DAVE HOGAN
first took pictures at the age of ten and went on to a two-year foundation course in Art, Photography and Design when he left school. An urge to travel meant he never finished his degree course in Sculptural Ceramics, but he used the opportunity to improve his photography while fulfilling his wanderlust. His first professional post was as Press Photographer at a Butlin's holiday camp, moving on via London's night clubs to covering film premieres and pop for the gossip column in the *Sun*. He has now been with the *Sun* for ten years, travelling worldwide while specialising in pop but also working on concerts and parties. Recent work has involved assignments on portraiture and book reviews for the *Sunday Telegraph*. He is currently working on a book which looks back at pop music in the eighties.

SIMON HOGGART
worked as the Northern Ireland correspondent for *The Guardian* from 1971 to 1973 before becoming Political Correspondent until 1977. From there he moved on to become a writer for *The Observer* in 1981 and then took up the role of their US correspondent between 1985 and 1989. His book *America — A Users' Guide* was published in 1990.

HRH THE DUKE OF YORK
bought himself a camera in the spring of 1983, his interest in photography having been aroused when he had been partly responsible for flying a photographer around Belize during military exercises. His pictures first appeared in an exhibition in October 1983 when he was asked to contribute to Personal Points of View — all the photographs were taken by people who were themselves the subjects of photographers. Since then his camera has been on many trips — both Royal and naval.

ROGER HUTCHINGS
studied documentary photography before moving to London in 1982 to begin his career as a freelance photographer. Since then he has covered social affairs, current affairs and general editorial work both nationally and internationally, for a wide range of clients. Represented by Katz Pictures, his work has appeared in, among others, *The Observer, The Guardian, US News World Report*, the *Telegraph Magazine* and the *Observer Magazine*. He is currently working on documentary projects.

SURESH KARADIA
studied architecture for four years before spending another two years studying photography at Art College in Gloucestershire. After college he assisted photographers in London while at the same time doing freelance work for *The Times* and *The Sunday Times*. From 1986 to 1988 he worked for *The Independent* and since then has worked on a freelance basis.

HERBIE KNOTT
had his first photographs published in the student newspaper *Cherwell* while he was

reading PPE at University College, Oxford. Before going freelance in 1975 he led a varied career which included reading for the Bar, working as a transport management trainee and cooking breakfasts for Irish navvies. Between 1977 and 1980 he worked mainly for the *London Evening Standard*, then *Now!* magazine and then on to the *Sunday Times* in 1981, where he stayed until 1986. In August of that year he was invited to join *The Independent* as a contract freelance and is still there today. His work illustrated the book *Diary of an Election* in 1983 and his own book, *Black and White,* is due to be published by Boxtree in October 1990. Current interests range from fashion, general news and feature coverage for *The Independent* to producing corporate photography for companies.

JOHN KOBAL

comes from Canada but has lived most of his life in London. He is an author, film historian, photo archivist, broadcaster, journalist and exhibition organiser. His collection of prints, negatives and other original film material is considered one of the most complete and important in the world and has been a source of major international exhibitions. He has written many books about Hollywood including biographies of Rita Hayworth, Marilyn Monroe and Marlene Dietrich and major studies of the work of the men who photographed the stars. His book, *People Will Talk* was greeted with rave reviews on both sides of the Atlantic and is currently being re-published as a paperback by Aurum for autumn 1990.

BARRY LEWIS

became bored with life as a chemistry teacher and so spent two years studying at the Royal College of Art to obtain his MA in Photography. He then started to work for *Vogue* magazine, where his growing reputation led to commissions from many other colour magazines. In 1981 he started the Network Photographers Agency with other photographers. Amongst other titles, his work has appeared in *Life* and the *Sunday Times Magazine,* and he now works mainly on projects for various books and

magazines. His awards include winning the GLC 'Portrait of a City' competition in 1979 and a 1986 commendation in the World Press Competition. He is currently working in the Eastern bloc countries covering the developments in Romania, East Germany and Albania.

ALISDAIR MACDONALD

left school to work in a commercial studio in London, then freelanced for west London local papers whilst working for a commercial studio in the West End. His coverage of the 1958 Notting Hill riots saw his pictures appear in the *Daily Mirror*. He freelanced for another year and joined the *Daily Mirror* as a staff photographer in 1960. When Robert Maxwell became its proprietor, he left after 26 years to join the *Today* newspaper.

EAMONN MCCABE F.R.P.S.

was the sports photographer for *The Observer* for over ten years before moving on to become picture editor of the short-lived *Sportsweek* magazine in 1986. Amongst his many awards are Sports Photographer of the Year for 1978, 1979, 1981 and 1984 and News Photographer of the Year in 1985. He has been picture editor at *The Guardian* since 1988 and was a Fellow in Photography at the National Museum of Photography, Film and Television at Bradford the same year.

TREVOR MCDONALD

he joined ITN in 1973 as a reporter. In 1978/79 he went as a Sports Correspondent to Australia to cover the English cricket tour. In 1980 he was appointed as ITN's Diplomatic Correspondent, taking that title to Channel Four News in 1982, becoming Diplomatic Editor in 1987. He covered world affairs, including reports from the 1984 Democratic convention in San Francisco and a visit to South Africa. His coverage of the Philippines in February 1986 won a BAFTA award for Channel Four News. Since March 1989 he has been presenting News at Ten and will continue to travel and report on special programmes. He began his television career in his native Trinidad in 1962 where he was an interviewer for the local current

affairs programmes Panorama and Dialogue. In 1969 he joined the BBC in London, first as a producer of current affairs programmes in the Caribbean Service, then producing World Service material. He lives in London and Devon: his hobbies include cricket and he has written biographies of Viv Richards and Clive Lloyd.

MIKE MALONEY F.R.P.S.

left school in Lincoln to embark on his intended career as an industrial chemist but left soon afterwards when he realised that chemistry was not for him. He joined his local weekly newspaper, the *Lincolnshire Chronicle,* to begin his career in photography and then moved to the London News Service. The post of show business photographer with the *London Evening News* followed, and in 1975 he was invited to join the *Daily Mirror* as their youngest staff man. His 40 major photographic awards include one as Photographer of the Year and he was made a Fellow of the Royal Photographic Society in 1986.
He is currently personal photographer to publishing magnate Robert Maxwell and chief photographer for *Mirror Group Newspapers.*

BOB MARTIN

joined the Allsport photographic agency after four years at Imperial College as a photographic trainee. He started as a darkroom junior progressing through to junior photographer and on to photographer. He then joined the Sporting Pictures agency which, after ten months, was followed by a short period of freelancing. Two years later he returned to Allsport. He likes to photograph almost anything and is especially interested in solving technical problems. He has collected 12 awards during his career

LEO MASON

moved into sports photography after a successful career in advertising. He spent a short period on the staff of *The Observer* in 1977, leaving to pursue a freelance career where he was able to do things his own way, and to make his own decisions. Among the many events he has covered are the last four Olympic Games, three soccer World Cup

finals tournaments, four Commonwealth Games and the 1983 and 1987 America's Cups. His work regularly appears in a variety of publications; *Time, Sports Illustrated, Stern* and *Paris-Match* and among his awards he has twice won the colour section in the British Sports Photographer of the Year Awards. He formed the Split Second sports photography agency in 1987 and is now fully occupied in running this expanding company with photographers Chris Cole and Tony Henshaw.

RICHARD MILDENHALL

started as an assistant to a theatre photographer in 1974 and then went on to work in fashion and advertising. After a period studying law and later dressage, he returned to photography. In 1985 he started working for *The Observer* and won the Nikon Photographic Award for his picture of the Brixton riots. In 1987 he won the Arts Photographer of the year award. He is still working for the Observer and has regular assignments from the Royal Shakespeare Company and the National Theatre.

DOD MILLER

is a freelance photographer who has worked for various national and international newspapers and magazines. His coverage of the Romanian revolution for *The Observer* in December 1989 won him a prize in the 1990 World Press Photography Awards.

DARIO MITIDIERI

came to London in 1982 and started working part-time at IDAF as a printer and at the Image Bank Picture Library. In 1985 he attended a one year course in photo-journalism at the London College of Printing which gave him more confidence in his work. Having freelanced for *The Times Educational Supplement, The Sunday Telegraph* and *The Independent,* he now works on British and foreign magazines and is a member of Select Photos Agency which syndicates his photographs worldwide. He is working on a documentary on slavery in the world today. In 1989 he won the title of News Photographer of the Year at the British Press Awards for his photograph of the massacre in Tiananmen Square.

DAVID MODELL
started freelancing for various small magazines and then the *Sunday Telegraph* newspaper. He worked there for two years and left a year ago and now works mainly for magazines. He is especially interested in black and white picture series.

ADRIAN MURRELL
began his career as a freelance sports photographer and, after covering the England tour to India in 1977, decided to specialise in cricket. He was special photographer for the *Cricketer International* magazine for ten years and now contributes regularly to *Cricket Life International*. His work has also appeared in numerous other publications (books, magazines and newspapers). In 1981 he was Ilford Sports Photographer of the Year and in 1985 won the Benson and Hedges Cricket Photographer of the Year Award. He was also highly commended for his 1977 and 1985 portfolios entered for the Sports Council/Royal Photographic Society Sports Photographer of the Year award. He joined the Allsport photographic agency in 1979 and in 1986 became Managing Director of Allsport UK.

GENE NOCON
first worked for a magazine during army service when he had to photograph a General in the US Army. After moving to England from America in 1975 he set up his own printing laboratory in London's Covent Garden. He won the Ilford Printer of the Year Award in 1985 establishing himself as one of London's best printers. He photographed The Duke and Duchess of York for the commemorative stamp of their engagement in 1986. He is also photographic adviser to HRH The Duke of York.

NORMAN PARKINSON O.B.E.
died on 14th February 1990 at Mount Elizabeth Hospital, Singapore, after a brief illness following a brain haemorrhage. Thus ended a long and distinguished career in photography which had had its beginnings in 1931 when he was apprenticed to Speaight & Son of Bond Street — a firm of court photographers. In 1934, with Norman Kibblewhite as his partner, the Norman Parkinson studio was opened, specialising in portraiture. The following year he started to work on a regular basis for both *Harper's Bazaar* and *The Bystander* and in 1942 his long association with *British Vogue* began. In 1949 his work appeared for the first time in *American Vogue* and continued to do so until the early sixties, when he became Associate Editor of *Queen* — the most influential fashion and features magazine of the time. 1963 saw his move from Twickenham to a dream-home in Tobago and in 1964, when his contract with *Queen* expired, he returned to working for both *Vogue* magazines as well as freelancing for *Life* and others. The late sixties saw his first official Royal portraits published — a connection which remained until his death and which saw him become a favourite of the HM Queen Elizabeth the Queen Mother. In the last year of his life he was still very active, with on-going projects for *Moda* in Italy, France and Sicily and for *Town & Country* in Israel, Spain, the USA, Barbados and Malaysia.

STEVE POWELL
joined the Keystone Press Agency straight from school. His first interest was photo-journalism and while at Keystone he was sent to cover events in Northern Ireland. In 1970 he met and started working with sports photographer Tony Duffy, the following year joining him at the Allsport photographic agency full-time. He went on to develop his career in sports photography, working for many international magazines — notably *Sports Illustrated* — specialising in athletics and winter sports. His work has been highly commended in numerous sports photography awards and he was winner of the American Best Sports Story Award in 1982 and Colour Sports Photographer of the Year in 1985. He is presently Allsport Group Managing Director.

ED PRITCHARD
entered photography in 1968 after three years at Birmingham College of Art. He freelanced for newspapers and magazines before a brief spell in a staff job on the *Daily Express*. Since then he has always worked for himself, mainly in the fields of advertising and corporate work, now working from a studio in Covent Garden.

CHRIS SMITH
started work for his local paper in Hartlepool, the *Northern Daily Mail*, at the age of 16. In the early sixties he moved to London to take up a job with the *Daily Herald*, where he gradually began to specialise in sports photography. He subsequently spent 8 years with *The Observer* and 13 years with *The Sunday Times* as a sports photographer, during which time he has won a succession of awards. Voted overall winner of Sports Photographer of the Year four times in a ten-year period, he has also had numerous highly-commended entries, and was winner of the Black and White Portfolio category in 1987. In 1989 he was voted the Expert's Expert by the *Observer Magazine*. His first book, *Sport in Focus*, was published in 1987 and in 1989 he co-authored *Boxing: The Champions* with Ken Jones.

JOHN STURROCK
first worked in the photography business for *Report*, covering assignments as a reportage photographer under the revered and veteran director Simon Guttman, in the seventies. At the same time he was also taking pictures for the *Socialist Worker* newspaper, a commitment he has remained faithful to throughout his career. In 1981 he and several other freelance photographers joined together to form the Network Photographer Agency and his interest in the development of the organisation remains active. Throughout the eighties he continued to cover social and political issues — an interest which resulted in his book *Blood, Sweat and Tears*, covering the events of the 1984-85 Miners' Strike. He is at present working on a long-term project on the effects of drug dependency, HIV infection, and unemployment on young people in the Muirhouse district of Edinburgh.

ALLAN TITMUSS
read Chemistry at London University, and English Language and Literature at Newcastle. He worked in industrial research and development and then as an arts administrator, founding and directing Newcastle's Literature Festival.
An unfinished PhD on contemporary British drama led to work in the theatre, quite accidentally to photographing plays, and very accidentally to photographing concerts. Probably best known for his music photographs in *The Guardian*, he specialises in arts photography, and his work appears in the press and on book jackets and record sleeves in the UK, Europe and the USA. In 1987, the first year the award was given, he was named British Arts Photographer of the Year for his photographs in *The Observer*.

IAN WOOLDRIDGE
was Cricket Correspondent for *The Daily Mail* for seven years before becoming its sports columnist in 1971. Since then he has twice been Columnist of the Year and four times Sports Writer of the Year in the British Press Awards and three times Sports Feature Writer of the Year in the Sports Council Awards. The most recent of his six books, *Sport in the Eighties*, is published by Centurion.

Trevor McDonald

In the summer of 1985, perhaps significantly right in the middle of the decade of the eighties, a pop concert linked across the Atlantic by satellite and seen by people in every corner of the world, raised nearly forty million pounds for the starving in famine stricken parts of Africa.

Live Aid, as the concert was known, became the event of the eighties.

With its simple and almost naively ambitious theme 'Feed the World', Live Aid raised money to buy and transport food to nourish hundreds of thousands of people from Ethiopia and the Sudan.

But it did much more than that, it cast a spell over a decade. It changed our perceptions of ourselves — we began the long road back towards a reaffirmation of our collective faith in human nature. In the devil-may-care, 'survival of the fittest' world of a morally debased Western society, Live Aid brought an injection of basic human decency.

In its wake it left the promises and actions of governments and politicians struggling for respectability. When, in the early months of the decade, Britain's Disasters Emergency Committee forecast that more than ten million people in East Africa would die because of drought, crop failures and local wars, it set out to raise a modest FIVE MILLION POUNDS. The response of the huge Common Market bureaucracy was more modest still. Brussels sent a mere three hundred thousand pounds' worth of drugs to Uganda.

Live Aid's imagination inspired us all to a much greater effort. It swung the focus back to the people, to the governed. That it was an idea born in the pop culture and made to work by rock idols made it all the more extraordinary. We, the observers of the changing patterns of life in the eighties, had come to think of these stars as hell-raising corrupters of the young, who polarised and incensed public opinion. Their involvement in promoting and staging Live Aid did the opposite. It *united* our global village.

Largely uncontroversial, it caused little debate. It didn't seek to blame anyone for the plight of the starving. It tried instead to help ease a burden made unbearable by years of neglect; it sought to soothe raw suffering with spontaneous compassion.

After Live Aid, that numbing complacency which nurtures so much inaction, began to die. In its place, a new awareness came alive.

In the spirit of what seemed a new age, it made assisting others less fortunate than ourselves popular again; it made raising money for causes possible, and not just those decreed and approved by the dead hand of government — AIDS, Sickle Cell Anaemia, victims of man-made and natural disasters.

Equally as fascinating as the Live Aid phenomenon was the way in which the problem it tackled was brought to the attention of the world.

It came by television, a medium which had come to be regarded as a provider of cheap entertainment, the epicentre of the cultural ghetto.

A television report described the famine in Ethiopia as one of almost biblical proportions and shocked us as we tucked into our evening meal. Those images so full of pain and suffering were the genesis of Live Aid's call to action.

More recently, television showed the awakening

and change of thousands of East Europeans. That coverage gave television in Britain a new dimension. We finally caught up with the Americans, and their tradition of employing it as a campaigning medium. 20 years ago, the first stirrings of the call to end America's involvement in Vietnam had some basis in political ideology, but it became an irresistible force only when American television embraced the cause. Americans had been told by their leaders that they were fighting the spread of communism in South East Asia; they weren't told about the cost in American lives, or about the grisly, bombing campaigns sedulously planned in Washington and callously executed against the people of Vietnam and Cambodia. Confronted on television by the reality of a brutal, unwinnable war against fighting foe and innocent peasants alike, the best intentions of presidents and Pentagon sank in a chorus of execration. The call to bring American troops home became an unstoppable emotional flood. Later in American politics, television had helped to bring down presidents and change the course of the nation, as well as end the Vietnam war.

In Britain, we too were learning its use in tapping the national mood and in summoning national resolve. We too began to see the medium as the bearer of the message.

Less profoundly, we became addicted to American 'soaps'. One of the biggest television audiences of all time in Britain was the one which watched one particular episode of the American soap opera Dallas to discover 'who killed JR'.

If Dallas was the opium of our adult masses, an alien creature named ET, accidentally abandoned on earth, became the cinematic love of millions of children.

We became more like America too in other aspects of life in the eighties. In scenes reminiscent of America's 'long hot summers' of the sixties, British towns and cities exploded in the worst outbreaks of civil unrest this century.

In Liverpool, Wolverhampton, Hull, Preston, Birmingham, Luton, Reading and London, young people ran riot through the streets during several nights of arson, looting and confronting the police.

These incidents bore heavily on the national conscience, demanding reponses other than the obvious knee-jerk 'law and order' reactions. Was it unemployment? Did poor housing and urban decay have a part to play? More ominously still, questions were raised about racism and police harassment.

We've still not honestly faced up to those questions. The unrest did more than pose a challenge to the civil authority. It brought us face to face with a new violence of our times, and with the fact that our society was split by deep divisions. It became impossible to ignore the fact that in truth, large sections of the population had become disaffected. They felt left out, uncared for, with no sense of belonging. Henceforth we would ignore them at our peril.

Television faced its own big challenge in the eighties... to make sense of the changes sweeping Eastern Europe. In Poland and Hungary, in Czechoslovakia and in East Germany, old ideologies and ideologues lost their grip on their countries.

Peacefully or in bloody insurrections, old orders disappeared.

In a way it all began in Moscow. Mr Gorbachev replaced a long line of ageing Soviet leaders, and embarked on a bold and controversial venture to drag the Union of Soviet Socialist Republics into the twentieth century.

Gorbachev, unlike the succession of grey men who preceeded him, saw the potential in using the medium. He decided that a measure of populism was needed if his revolution in glasnost and perestroika were to succeed. So out into the country he went, plunging into crowds arguing, urging, trying desperately to convince his people about a new course for their country. He went to East/West summit meetings and enjoyed entertaining Ronald Reagan in Moscow. He'd embraced that questionable philosophy of the American television 'photo opportunity'.

All the while, Gorbachev was using television to explode old ideas, outdated forms of management and control which had palpably failed.

But more than anything he accomplished at home, he gave his assent to change in Eastern Europe. When he gave that signal, television captured the most memorable images of the decade... hundreds of thousands of people converging on the Berlin Wall, ready to pull it down with the sheer weight of their passion and joy, were it not for the fact that the leaders of East Germany had already assured the world the wall *was* about to come down.

In Romania, thousands of people gathered in the main square in Bucharest and shouted down a bewildered Nicolae Ceaucescu, beginning a process which sent him and his wife to ignominious deaths and ended his ruinous dictatorship. The bloody battles between the Romanian old guard and the advocates of people power provided television journalism with compelling images.

By the end of the decade, the begetter of the change himself, Mr Gorbachev was heading for trouble. Discontent in the Soviet Baltic republics and an economy unable to meet the demand of its consumers, threatened his presidency.

It had all happened before in the Soviet Union, but this time there was one important difference — Mr Gorbachev couldn't hide his problems — this time they were all out in the open. Television had seen to that.

As the decade began, police in Turin fired tear gas to quell a riot started by English football fans. It had begun on the ground and later spilled onto the streets. No one advanced any new thoughts about football hooliganism, and no one could doubt that it acquired a frightening momentum in the eighties.

A stunned England soccer manager talked of our collective 'shame'. It was a description which would come up again and again all through a sad chronology of events during the eighties.

If the single mindedness of soccer hooligans gave rise to the feeling that there was something sinister and sick festering away in the deepest recesses of our national being, the spirit provoked by the battle for the Falklands was perceived by the majority to be vastly different. A war to reclaim a group of barren, largely forsaken islands eight thousand miles from home united the nation as never before. There was some dissent, but it was easily swamped by a bull-dog demonstration of national resolve. And he who had no stomach for the fight had little choice but to depart. The islands had been invaded by Argentina, contrary to every code of international political manners and they *had* to be reclaimed. And if in the process Argentina was made to pay a price for its transgression, then so be it. We should all 'Rejoice'. The Falklands campaign said a lot about the England of the eighties — it was perhaps, the country's definitive vote.

Britain had lost considerable power and influence in the world — according to some observers, not always unkindly disposed, it still had not found a compensating role — and had grown indecisive.

But some things had *not* changed, even in the age of consumerism, conspicuous wealth, and the flabbiness brought about by gracious living.

Behind all the trappings of modernity, there still lurked that old, proud British spirit, shaped in the crucible of ancient wars, toughened by stirring memories of the few who did so much for so many, and unforgiving in matters of setting certain wrongs to right. The resolve to retake the islands in the South Atlantic blew away the cobwebs of history.

'When the blast of war blows in our ears,
Then imitate the action of the tiger;
Stiffen the sinews, summon up the blood,
Disguise fair nature with hard favour'd rage.'

That was as much the tone of the eighties as it had

been the call to arms in Henry V. Britain in the eighties embraced the silicon chip but it had not forgotten its past. It was no longer a world power but a frequently prickly member of a rapidly expanding European Community and largely subservient to the interests of the United States.

But going to war over the Falklands gave the country and its leaders a chance to remember old times again and for a brief and shining moment to recreate the greatness of Drake, Nelson and Shakespeare.

Roger Hutchings

A crowd gathered in Wenceslas Square, calling for the resignation of the communist government.

Prague, Czechoslovakia 24th November 1989

Dod Miller

Revolution in Eastern Europe as the eighties end. In Palace Square the army joined with the people to oust the hated Ceaucescu regime.

Bucharest, Romania 23rd December 1989

Dod Miller

Romanian revolution. Soldiers under heavy Securitate sniper fire in the side streets off Palace Square.

Bucharest, Romania 23rd December 1989

Dod Miller

Romanian revolution. The funeral of young student Valentina Pandele — killed by a Securitate sniper's bullet on the way to visit her father.

Bercini Village, near Bucharest, Romania Christmas Day 1989

Eamonn McCabe

6 am. I came across this bizarre scene as if from a movie.

Soweto Township near Johannesburg, South Africa 1979

Nobby Clark

**Cadlington House — a Mencap home for
mentally handicapped children.**

Horndean, Hampshire 1984

Roger Hutchings

Opposite, taken in Naruse camp in Southern
Sudan. This was a camp controlled by the Sudan
Peoples Liberation Army which for 10 years has
been fighting the forces of the Muslim
government in the North. I went there to report
the war, and the allegations that both sides were
using food as a weapon to control the inhabitants
of the area. This boy was at a feeding station. This
makeshift sun vizor was the only toy he had.

Naruse Camp, Sudan October 1986

David Modell

Children playing in a lake, right.
Site 2, Cambodian refugee camp.

Thai/Cambodian border, September 1987

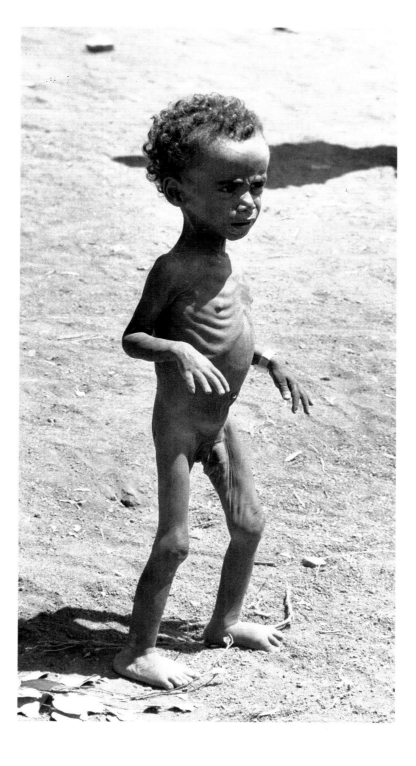

Kent Gavin

I have visited many countries in which there has been evidence of dreadful starvation during my career but this particular fight for life was appalling. This little boy, right, died two hours after this photo was taken. The shock was more of an impact to me than I had ever experienced as it was the children who were dying in their thousands. The little girl, opposite, was carrying her dying brother to a field hospital in an attempt to get food and medical treatment. I will never forget the look of hopelessness on her face.

Bati, Ethiopia
8th November 1984

Dave Hogan

Sting, far right, pictured at the Live Aid concert showing what a long day it had been. That day I had 13 cameras around my neck as I was one of the official photographers for the book, covering backstage, front of house, dressing rooms and the royal box. At the end of the day I decided never again to work with so many cameras as I got so confused and couldn't remember which camera related to which newspaper and/or magazine.

Wembley Stadium, North London
July 1985

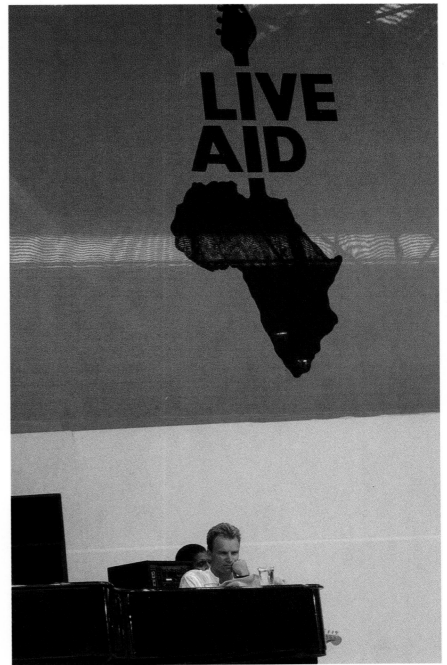

Julian Calder

The ferret judge, left. Shot on 35mm, the perfect close-working lens, which provides just enough physical contact between the subject and the photographer and positions the subject in his environment.

Lowther Fair, Cumbria 1985

Suresh Karadia

Tender Touch.
A young visitor, opposite, to the Exploring Woodland and Seashore exhibition for the Blind at the Natural History Museum, Kensington, strokes the fur of a rabbit she will never see. The animals seemed to have a sixth sense when amongst the children and people who suffer from this disability and act with complete calm throughout.

London 1st March 1983

Alisdair MacDonald

**Identity Parade.
Minstrel the cat, below,
who lives at the police dog
training school, puts them
to the test.**

*Keston, Kent
18th June 1987*

Sally Fear

Dog psychologist, left.

London 1979

Richard Cooke

I was taking general views of people using the Lea Valley Park when suddenly this little boy ran up covered in calamine lotion and full of *joie de vivre*, stopped for a second to have his picture taken and then ran off laughing.

London July 1981

Alisdair MacDonald

This is one of the Crufts cliche´
pictures. On the first day of the
show one always takes a
selection of pictures that have
all been done before —
fortunately the desk men's
memories are not very good.
Other pictures could be: Child
asleep in dog's box; Back view
of man with his arm around a
blonde (Afghan); Dog and dog
owner lookalikes.

Earls Court, London
12th February 1988

Tim Graham

In the queue in Tiananmen Square, Beijing, waiting to visit Mao's tomb. This picture was taken during the Queen's historic visit to China — a couple of days later the Queen was in the square to inspect a guard of honour with President Li as part of the official welcoming ceremony.

Beijing, China October 1986

NO SMOKING

David Modell

The Northern Line, opposite, a commuters' Hell.
Part of a sequence portraying life underground during
the rush hour.

London 1988

Richard Mildenhall

Above, Mother and son herding their bullocks.

Near Galway, Eire 13th December 1985

Mike Abrahams

The Young Conservatives Ball.

London 1986

Sally Fear

Morgan Grenfell dealing room during the flotation of British Airways.

London 1987

Roger Hutchings

Girl sniffing glue during a political rally above, and right, Christmas time in Trafalgar Square.

Manchester July 1981 and London 28th December 1987

Eamonn McCabe

Heysel Stadium, left.
I took this very early as the wall broke. It is a sound
I will never forget, hearing a man calling for his friend,
surrounded by the shoes of those who had died on the
terraces, 'Mario, Mario'.

European Cup Final, Liverpool v Juventus
Brussels 29th May 1985

Chris Smith

Roma fans, above, at the European Cup Final.

Rome 1984

HRH The Duke of York

One of a series of Norfolk churches.

Castle Rising, Norfolk 30th December 1985

Gene Nocon

My first visit to London.

Westminster, London 1979

Richard Mildenhall

**Roller skaters during the
Brixton riots.**

*South London
28th September 1985*

John Sturrock

The miners' strike.
Left, mass picket at Orgreave coke works.
Below, the police are pushed over their own front line at Kellingley Colliery.

Sheffield, Yorkshire 30th May 1984, left and below, near Pontefract, Yorkshire 10th September 1984

Kent Gavin

After visiting a pub in South London, left, where a drag show was taking place
I witnessed just this event which gave me a big laugh — I then thought: 'Well how does a drag artist spend a penny?' My creative imagination thought up the character on the left, and I had to find a clean toilet to stage the picture in with models, great fun.

London
20th September 1980

Herbie Knott

Opposite, Olgli Likhovskaya of the Kirov Ballet based in Leningrad shot just before a photo-call with children whilst she was removing her leggings.

Business Design Centre
Islington, London
22nd July 1988

Suresh Karadia

Above, French fashion designer Claude Montana's ready to wear autumn/winter Collection.

Cour Carree du Louvre, Paris March 1986

Jill Furmanovsky

Vivienne Westwood's show, opposite, shot for *The Face* magazine.

Olympia, London 31st March 1981

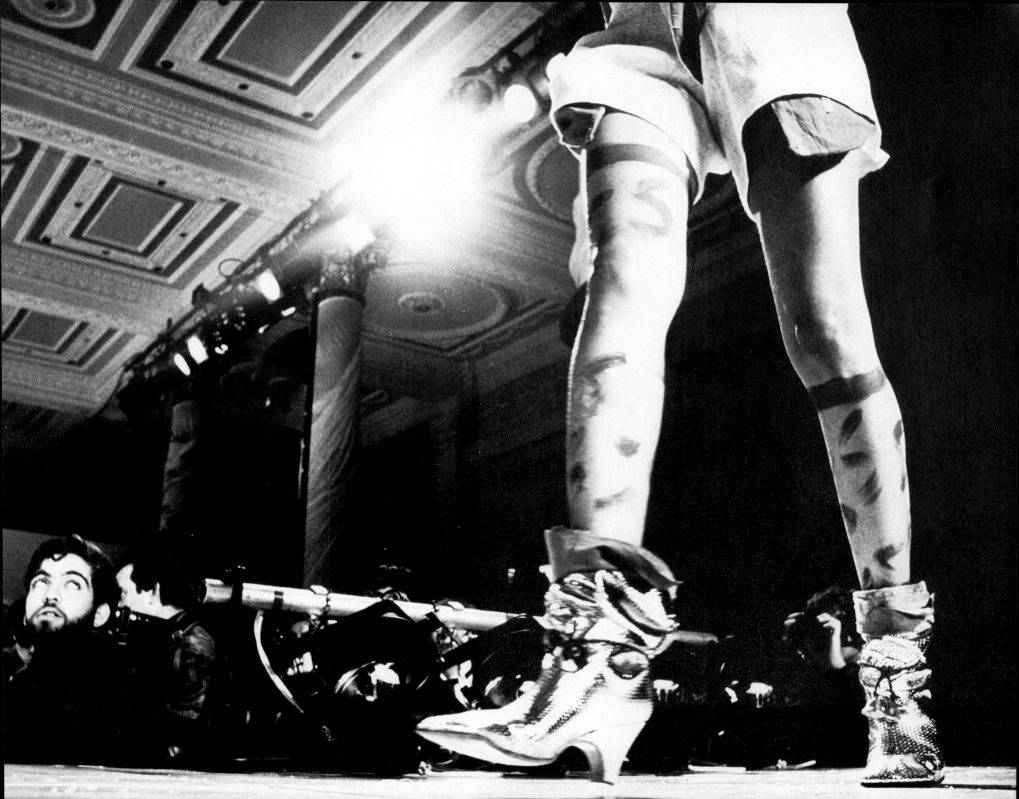

Suresh Karadia

Fashion designer Jean Paul Gaultier's spring/summer Collection.

London 1989

Norman Parkinson

The Duchess of Feria is a dressage expert and coaxed her horse, Marchioness of Villa Alba, into posing with her for this photograph.

Barbados, West Indies 1982

Alisdair MacDonald

This was the coldest day since records began, -16 degrees Centigrade. After the snow had stopped it was found that Kent had been hit the worst.
A helicopter loaded down with Fleet Street photographers set off to hunt for pictures. After looking at Sheppey and Ashford we discovered Sittingbourne High Street. I took the Lowry-type pictures and returned to Battersea Heliport. With four photographers in the helicopter we all took turns to stick our lenses out of a 8" x 6" sliding window. Because it was so cold we kept the door on.

Sittingbourne, Kent
12th January 1987

Herbie Knott

The funeral of Station Officer Colin Townsley, who died in the King's Cross Underground fire.

Covent Garden, London November 1987

Roger Hutchings

In the Milltown cemetery I saw a stone mason carving the names of the 'Gibraltar Three' on the Republican memorial stone.

West Belfast, Northern Ireland March 1988

Herbie Knott

A Battle of Britain dispersal airfield, above, re-created by Jane Coleman for the WW2 drama series, 'Piece of Cake' shot for LWT.

Friston, East Sussex June 1988

Richard Cooke

This picture of the Red Arrows team was taken by removing the brake parachute from a Hunter and fitting a specially designed camera enabling me to operate it from inside the aircraft via the brake parachute release button. The story behind this photograph was the subject of a television programme, 'The Moment of Truth'.

Lincolnshire April 1985

Ed Pritchard

Commissioned by the GLC, this picture (shot just before a thunderstorm) is one of many I took in various lighting conditions for the book commemorating the opening of the Thames Barrier in 1984.

London 1984

Richard Cooke

This photograph was for a magazine piece on the Indian Pacific Railway from Sydney to Perth, a journey of two and a half days. The Nullarbor Plain section takes most of one day. There is no scenery at all.

Western Australia September 1982

David Modell

Blackpool night club — two dancing couples with an audience.

Blackpool, Lancashire April 1989

David Modell

The widow of Daniel McCann is sheltered from the Loyalist attack during his funeral at the Milltown cemetery.

West Belfast, Northern Ireland March 1988

David Modell

Opposite, digging the English end of the Channel Tunnel.

Folkestone, Kent March 1989

Dario Mitidieri

Kumba Mela Festival, above. Approximately 15 million pilgrims had a holy bath in a single day during the festival which celebrates the 'Sungam' or meeting point of the Ganges and the Yamuna River in Allahabad every 12 years.

Allahabad, India 6th February 1989

Dario Mitidieri

Tehran, right. The Iran/Iraq war is over, but the street paintings are still a powerful means of political and religious propaganda.

Tehran, Iran November 1988

Martin Cleaver

Man being beaten by soldiers, above. This is one of a series of photographs of the 'Intifada' which contributed to my receiving a serious beating by the Israeli Defence forces.

Ramallah, Occupied West Bank March 1988

Roger Hutchings

Benazir Bhutto on the campaign trail. It was obvious that she had massive support, with hysterical crowds mobbing her wherever she went.

Punjab, Pakistan November 1988

Dario Mitidieri

Three days before the massacre of Tiananmen Square an excited crowd applauds the unveiling of the statue 'The Goddess of Liberty' which became the symbol of the Democratic movement.

Beijing, China 1st June 1989

Dario Mitidieri

**Despite continuous firing, students keep a close watch
on the army occupation of Tiananmen Square.**

Beijing, China 4th June 1989

Dario Mitidieri

An injured soldier, below, is taken away to safety after his tank was destroyed in Tiananmen Square, while opposite, bodies delivered to the 'Capital Hospital' give the lie to government claims that no one was killed in the Square.

Beijing, China 4th June 1989

Roger Hutchings

This was a shrine in Narodni Street, marking where a student had been killed by the riot police. The revolution was essentially started by students and young people, but slowly the older generation, frightened and stifled during the 20 years since the Prague Spring 1968, began to show their support. Mainly young people were coming to this shrine, but I noticed this old man standing on the edge of the crowd. He seemed slightly reticent and stood watching but after a while he came gingerly forward and stooped to place and light his candle.

Prague, Czechoslovakia 23rd November 1989

Mike Maloney

Lockerbie child, opposite.
I was driving home from a party when the picture editor rang me to tell of the crash and I immediately drove from London to Scotland. This little boy's grandfather had the luckiest of escapes when both houses either side of him were totally demolished. I decided to take the grandson to a local church for a prayer of thanks.

Lockerbie, Dumfries and Galloway, Scotland 22nd December 1988

Tim Graham

**Opposite, Remembrance Day,
The Cenotaph, Whitehall.**

London 13th November 1988

Sally Fear

**Mrs Ann West, above, whose daughter, Lesley
Ann Downey, aged 10, was one of the victims of
the Moors murderers on Boxing Day 1964.**

England 1986

Richard Mildenhall

Itinerant child selling holly from door to door, in the period running up to Christmas.

Cork, Eire 9th December 1985

Suresh Karadia

Remembrance. Men who were evacuated from Dunkirk in 1940 return to honour their fallen comrades.

Dunkirk Beach, Northern France 11th September 1987

Martin Cleaver

Above, HMS Antelope explodes in San Carlos Water. The explosion was so fast that by the second frame on the motor drive the detonation flash had gone. I still do not know how I managed to react so quickly. Opposite, HMS Hermes. This is a very strong composition which I saw by chance while awaiting a helicopter ride. I had to wait until the dawn over the flight deck balanced the fluorescent light in the hangar.

The Falkland Islands, South Atlantic April 1982

Martin Cleaver

Home.
One of the final shots of the war of the Argentine POWs going home — something I too was very much looking forward to.

Port Stanley, Falkland Islands June 1982

Alisdair MacDonald

Brize Norton airfield was visited every other day by Fleet Street during the Falklands War or so it seemed. Here, the Paras were returning to be met by Prince Charles. While he was in the scrum with the troops I took this shot. The child was only a bundle when dad went to war — on his return he could now walk.

Oxfordshire July 1982

Sally Fear

Opposite, the first survivors from HMS Sheffield arrive at Brize Norton airfield during the Falklands crisis.

Oxfordshire 13 May 1982

Barry Lewis

**The longest car in the world. A 67ft custom built Cadillac with 22 wheels. It cannot actually be driven.
It was bought by a Japanese businessman as an attraction to his health resort where he charges £2.50 a look.**

Osaka, Japan 1st September 1988

Julian Calder

Ed's Diner. Shot for *Business* magazine's guide to Chicago in their City Guide series. I have
photographed six cities for this series. I love this type of assignment as it gives you a week to ten
days to discover a place, plan and organise pictures but also to produce pure reportage pictures.

Chicago, USA 1988

Mike Maloney

This guardsman fainted under the blazing sun at the wedding of Prince Charles to Lady Diana Spencer.

London 29th July 1981

Jill Furmanovsky

Sleeping photographer.
This is one of the portrait
photographers who works in the
square by the church in Cuzco,
Peru. The people in Peru are
very shy and I took very few
portraits. The exception were
the photographers; I made a
point of commissioning a
portrait of myself (and friends)
if I saw one, and then I felt OK
about taking theirs.

Cuzco, Peru August 1983

Marcus Binney

Conservation poses the greatest new moral dilemma of our age. In the name of progress — for mankind rather than for any of the myriad species that share the earth with us — we have set in motion a chain of events that is making extinction an everyday event, and threatening the ecological equilibrium of the planet.

Scientists argue whether the greenhouse effect will melt the polar icecaps and submerge huge areas of the earth's surface. Experts dispute whether acid rain is causing the death of forests, lakes and rivers. But for the individual the fundamental dilemma is becoming more apparent every passing week. Is it right that man, to improve his own lot, should destroy the means of existence, the food and the habitat of other species?

Darwin's theory of the survival of the fittest provided a convenient ethical justification to thrust the engine of progress forward at full throttle. The idea of progress has had a ready, easily grasped justification, in the great advances in medicine, hygiene and living conditions for millions of people. The successful fight against disease, lower child mortality rates, longer lifespans, can all be counted as achievements for progress. Those species which could not compete were supposedly succumbing to a natural process — even if, like the American plains buffalo, death was speeded by a hail of bullets. In the last decade the public at large has become increasingly aware that there is nothing natural about what man is doing to the planet.

Few of us, at least in the West, have yet reached the stage where we believe it is wrong to kill a fly, but we are deeply concerned that thousands of species of flora and fauna are becoming extinct or being reduced below genetically sustainable numbers. Opposition to hunting, to fur coats and snakeskin bags, outcry about animal welfare and factory farming all reflect concern about cruelty and damage to other species.

The Green Consumer movement, the vast increase in media coverage of Green issues, show this is happening. In the course of a few years we have witnessed a fundamental change in people's attitude to the world around them. A few years ago anyone arguing that industry should adopt more environmentally friendly processes of production was always told this: people simply wanted the goods at the cheapest possible price. Whether this meant battery chickens, or bigger lorries, the litany was always the same: people would not pay the added cost of more effective environmental policies. In a matter of months rather than years this has been overturned. Millions have led the way in turning to additive-free food in supermarkets. Millions have changed to lead-free petrol.

One of the most acute problems today remains that those who most need to practise conservation are those least able to afford it. Rainforests are destroyed in the main not by rapacious capitalist timber merchants, but by poor people desperate for agricultural land to provide food and escape starvation. In the island of Haiti there is so little fuel left that for many the only means of cooking is to marinate food in lemon juice. Similarly the most polluting industry is to be found in Eastern Europe, India and China.

Often these processes have been speeded up and landscape and wildlife destroyed because of supplies of aid and investment from the developed nations. The great guiding principle of the new conservation age should be to ensure that natural resources are not exhausted but renewed. We must put back as much goodness into the soil as we take out of it. Areas of rainforest which have been logged must be left alone and given the chance to regenerate. All rainforests nonetheless cannot be kept as virgin wilderness and protected as national parks or nature reserves. We must find ways by which they can provide a living for those who live there, and vital foreign exchange for the countries that must care for them. Logging is not new. What is needed is selective logging carried out in such a way that the minimum damage is done when the trees are extracted.

Conservation is an attitude of mind. It is centred on good stewardship of the earth's resources, whether natural or man-made. Before we destroy or alter the face of the world around us we need to think through the consequences. Hedgerows are not just obstacles to efficient farming, they provide a habitat for wildlife, and a windbreak that can reduce soil erosion. Pasture unsprayed provides the wildflowers that nourish the insects which feed the birds. Beneath ancient grassland a whole world of landscape archaeology is preserved — not just the waving outline of medieval ridge and furrow.

The threat to all forms of life, to the very biosphere on which all life depends, to the whole natural world as we know it, is posed by forces we have unleashed but which are now beyond our control. We do not know if we have the means to control the ever-widening hole in the atmosphere, the ozone layer, or to cope with nuclear accidents and nuclear waste. What is clear is that it is no longer sufficient to wait for the scientists to provide definitive proof of what is happening before we act. That will be too late. We have learnt to our cost that by the

time scientific proof of a destructive environmental process is forthcoming it may be too late to stop it. What is needed is a fundamental change in ethics. The good news is that this is happening. It has begun with millions of personal choices by individual consumers. This is having a major impact on business, both on the manufacture of products and the image companies seek to present of themselves.

Let us put the grandiose idea of the Conquest of Nature behind us. We need to cherish nature, not consistently assault it. Otherwise the James Bond catchline 'Live and let die' may prove to be the real epitaph of our age.

Mike Goldwater

Prey Veng paddy fields, above.
A sense of normality prevails after the horrors of the past.

Kampuchea, South East Asia 1988

Julian Calder

Wheat field, opposite.
Taken for Barclays Bank from a helicopter at sunset.

Wiltshire/Hampshire border 1989

Julian Calder

Swaledale from Crackpot Hill, the heart of Herriot country. I have spent eight years photographing Yorkshire for the James Herriot calendars. The weather is often against you, but there is always a picture to be had — even within a few yards of the car.

Yorkshire 1987

Tim Graham

Desert. Massive shifting sand dunes the size of hills.

Qatar, Persian Gulf February 1979

Heather Angel

I decided to crop in tight on this old orang-utan using the cheek flanges to frame the face. Not until I looked at the transparency on a light box did I realise I had caught someone else's flash highlights in the eyes.

San Diego Zoo, California, USA 8th January 1988

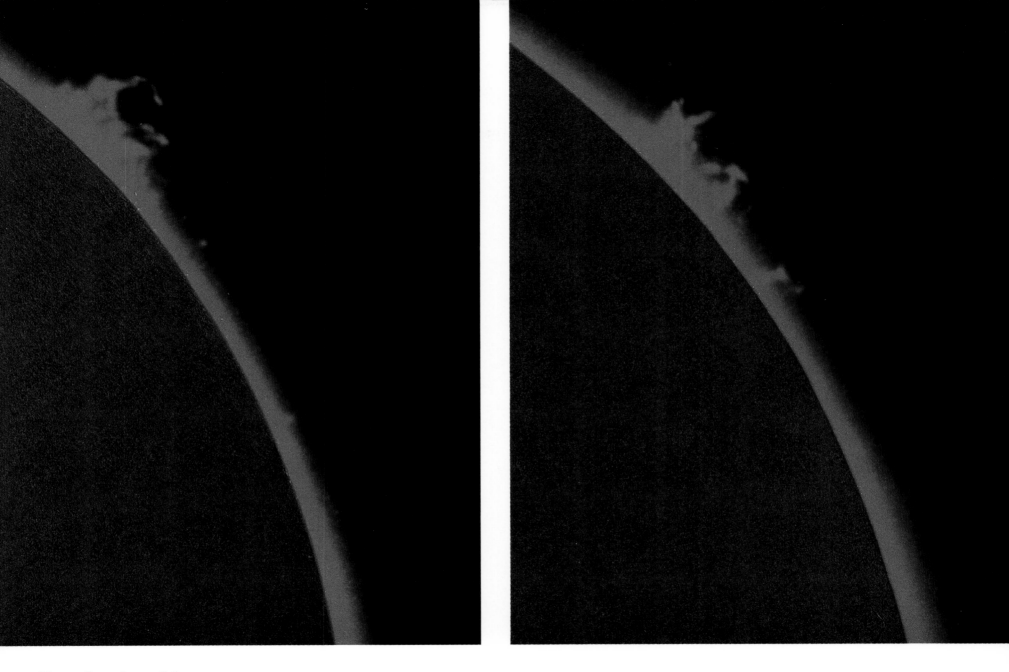

Douglas Arnold

Solar prominence. A composite slide of two images obtained using a DayStar hydrogen alpha filter. They record the development of a prominence over a 15-minute period.

27th November 1988

Jill Furmanovsky

Machu Picchu, Peru, left. I had no intention of photographing Machu Piccu. It was already well documented on postcards and anyway it was full of tourists. Suddenly it began to rain and everyone disappeared to take shelter, at the same time I realised I had the place to myself in perfect light and I went to work.

Andes Mountains, Peru August 1983

Heather Angel

Base of Svartifoss waterfall, opposite. I had already taken the conventional shot of the complete waterfall when I put on a 200mm lens to look at plants on high ledges. As I panned the camera round I saw this simple but graphic picture of the base of the waterfall.

Skaftafell National Park, Iceland 26th July 1981

Julian Calder

Vigorous protests saved the life of this seal pup, opposite, and many others.

*Orkney Islands
Scotland 1983*

Stephen Dalton

**Barn Owl.
I spent many weeks photographing a pair which had chosen to raise their offspring in an old clock tower on a private estate in Sussex. Most of the time was devoted to preparing the site and gradually getting the birds accustomed to all my photographic paraphernalia. As barn owls are becoming scarce, a special licence from the Nature Conservancy has to be obtained before photographing them at their nests.**

Ardingly, Sussex 1988

Stephen Dalton

Chameleon catching a butterfly. The chameleon is a creature which some people regard with apprehension. Certainly this fascinating animal has more than its fair share of bizarre attributes. In addition to its well-known ability to change colour within seconds, each eye can swivel through 180 degrees in any direction quite independently. Even its method of catching food is unconventional. This butterfly lived to see another day, as its wing-scales, which easily become detached, stuck to the tongue and the insect escaped.

Ardingly, Sussex 1979

Stephen Dalton

Brown Rat. The life of the brown rat was a self-appointed assignment and to effect some of the photography I was compelled to keep a number of these animals at home. Before long the whole family was totally captivated by their endearing qualities. The individual leaping out of the dustbin (Ratty was her name) hated the filth and stink of the rubbish and could not wait to jump out to get back into her clean and familiar cage. When Ratty eventually died, there was not a dry eye in the house.

Ardingly, Sussex 1982

Michael Busselle

Landscape with flowers and dark sky, above. Field of flowers, opposite.

Near Cuis, Marne, France February 1984 and near San Carcus del Valle, Ciudad Real, Spain May 1986

Herbie Knott

Frozen feet on a winter's morning in Richmond Park.
Mine, I mean.

London December 1981

Heather Angel

During a lull on a whale-watching cruise off Mexico's Baja California, I spotted this still life of sea fans and shells laid out to dry on the stern of our boat.

Magdalena Bay, Mexico 17th February 1988

Unity Hall

His Royal Highness Prince Philip, the Duke of Edinburgh, is on record as saying that if the British people wanted the Monarchy to go, they would go quietly. But the truth is that even in this changing decade of the twentieth century, to most people it is unthinkable that the Queen and her family would ever be asked to move on.

In the last decade public interest in the Monarchy has multiplied. The public appetite is insatiable for more information, more pictures, more news about the Queen and her family.

The last ten years have perhaps been the most significant of the Queen's 38-year reign. It was the marriage of her eldest son, the Prince of Wales, and the birth of Prince William and Prince Harry (assuring continuity of the Royal line) that stirred an interest and popularity that Royalty have not enjoyed since the Queen, at the age of 27, was crowned on 2nd June 1953.

Royal advisors sometimes fear that this intense curiosity trivialises the Monarchy. They feel that the apparent willingness of some of the younger members of the family to pander to the public, with television appearances and writing books, will destroy the mystique and therefore eventually undermine the delicate foundations on which the Monarchy survives. But the Queen is alert to these perils. Throughout her reign she has taken cautious but progressive steps towards modernising the Royal family while instilling in each and every member of it a sense of service to her subjects and the country.

The Royal decade began with the meeting of Prince Charles and Lady Diana Spencer, on the Royal Yacht at Cowes week in 1980. She caught the Prince of Wales's eye to such effect that in July 1981 they were married at St Paul's Cathedral.

While he was the first heir to the throne ever to marry a commoner, albeit one with aristocratic connections, Diana will not be the first commoner Queen of England. Charles's grandmother HM Queen Elizabeth the Queen Mother, 90 this year and as busy as ever, holds that record. When, as Lady Elizabeth Bowes-Lyon, she married the young Duke of York it was at a time when Royalty only married Royalty. But then no one dreamt that her Duke would ever become King. Had there been any suspicion that his elder brother, King Edward VIII, would abdicate (for the love of an American divorcee) it is doubtful that the Duke of York would ever have been given permission to marry the charming Elizabeth — the finest consort any King could have. Her favourite grandson's marriage to Lady Diana Spencer on 29th July 1981, was the Royal event of the eighties.

Five years later, in 1986, the Queen's second son, Prince Andrew, also married a commoner, the untitled, red-headed, hoydenish Sarah Ferguson who never attempted to hide a past which included other lovers.

Not all the recent times have been happy for the Monarchy. There was a time when divorce between those close to the throne was unthinkable. The Queen, as head of the Church of England, could not condone divorce. If a marriage failed, the couple went their own separate ways, careful not to cause scandal. But in this changing world, where one in three marriages fails, the Queen has reluctantly had to accept that her own family are not immune. In the last decade we have seen Princess Anne separated from her husband Captain Mark Phillips, and two years before the eighties began Princess Margaret shed her husband, Lord Snowdon.

All of these events, happy and sad, have one traditional

common factor. None could have taken place without the consent of the Queen.

Princess Anne's children were sent to the local village school near her home in Gloucestershire. Prince William is the first heir to the throne to be sent to nursery school, with Prince Harry following suit.

Bringing up Princes and Princesses is a complex task. They must be instilled with a sense of the mystery of the Monarchy and learn young that they are different and that for them there are different rules to follow. Their lives should be ones of duty to what is almost an abstract concept. The Queen's children have learned these lessons well, though some took longer than others. There are those who say that today Princess Anne is more Royal and more formal than the Queen herself. Charles, even while expressing forceful opinions of his own, has never so much as dented the dignity of the Monarchy. The younger sons, Andrew and Edward, had more freedom and therefore made more mistakes. But they, too, are now buckling down to dedicated lives of mature responsibility.

Though she dislikes having to interfere in her family's private lives and public activities, the Queen is Monarch first and mother second. Hers is the voice, in tune with that of her husband, which cautions, counsels and eventually declares enough is enough.

Her real problems have come with new arrivals into the family. For commoners, marriage to a Royal can at first be traumatic. The loss of personal freedom and lack of privacy hit hard. Newcomers have to learn painfully to live in the confinement that being Royal brings. In the early days of their marriages, both Princess Diana and the Duchess of York found themselves on the carpet in the Queen's study, being told to improve their ways.

There are those who complain that the Monarchy is expensive, but generally speaking the British do get a hardworking, dedicated Royal family in return for the taxpayers' money. Most of their work is done for charity and many of the working members of the family have increased their work-load. They are in great demand.

Princess Anne, with her amazing work for the Save the Children Fund, the Duchess of Kent with her involvement in hospices and Prince Philip's abiding interest in youth projects are all of incalculable value. Princess Diana, who at the beginning of her marriage began to acquire a reputation as a flibbertigibbet clothes-horse, is today the Royal family's finest asset. She has grown enormously in stature, her work-load is heavy, and the girl who found public speaking a torture now makes serious, meaningful speeches on subjects as diverse as marriage, child care and AIDS. She has charm, and the same quality that the Queen had as a young girl — the ability to show that she really cares.

And what of the nineties? By the end of them, the Queen will be 74. There are those who believe that long before then Her Majesty should step down in favour of Prince Charles. When the Prince of Wales does come to the throne he will not be inexperienced in the affairs of State. Since he was 18, the Queen has been training him for the day he is King. But what is certain is that the Queen will not abdicate. At her Coronation, she was crowned Queen and anointed Queen. This is of powerful, religious significance. When Edward VIII gave up the throne he did so before his coronation, and in the whole 1,000-year history of British Royalty a crowned monarch has never abdicated. The Queen is hardly likely to shatter such a record.

Mike Maloney

Standing at his full height of 6ft 4in, Lord Porchester, above, the Queen's racing manager, appears to be shorter than HM, normally 5ft 2in, who is jumping over a foot in the air with excitement watching the climax to the Derby.

Epsom, Surrey June 1980

Alisdair MacDonald

Opposite, I spent the night before the wedding on the pavement and after 16 hours leapt over the crush barrier and got to the Palace railings to get this shot.

Buckingham Palace 29th July 1981

Julian Calder

The Queen's visit to China. The Queen inspecting the Terracotta Warriors. This was the shot I wanted to take, so in preparation I carried fast film and a tripod throughout the trip — cumbersome luggage. *Life* magazine used this as their picture of the month.

Xian, China 1987

Tim Graham

The Queen caught in a cloudburst after the Trooping the Colour ceremony.

Buckingham Palace June 1982

Kent Gavin

Sarah Ferguson, as she then was, kissed and cuddled Prince Andrew and joked about the engagement. The Prince, being a photographer himself, laughed when asked to repeat a picture again. Prince Andrew asked why I had missed the kissing picture of Fergie. I then asked Fergie to kiss him again. He joked 'No', Fergie then gave him this loving look, Andrew heard the motordrive go and said 'I think you have it now'.

Buckingham Palace
19th March 1986

Alisdair MacDonald

Charles and Diana were at Buckingham Palace for William's christening. I was outside the Palace for four hours. This picture was taken as they left to go back to Kensington Palace after lunch. The baby is bawling its head off as Charles looks unhappy about the noise.

London 4th August 1982

Tim Graham

The Princess of Wales on a walkabout.

Munich, West Germany November 1987

Kent Gavin

Prince Charles running in the sea.
The Royal Protection officers from
London and Australia were taken by
surprise at Charles' fitness. Two days
later I was told at a reception with the
Prince, 'I was quite surprised you
managed to keep up with me'.
What he did not know was that I had
been there two days running and
watched his routine and pre-
positioned myself to get this picture.
This picture was taken after
arranging for a bikini-clad model,
Jane Priest, to kiss Prince Charles
after finishing swimming. Unknown
to Prince Charles the model was due
to take her bikini top off after
swimming with him. Charles was a
stronger swimmer and missed the
lovely Miss Priest topless — though
she did manage to kiss him later.

Gottesloe Beach, Perth
Western Australia
March 1979

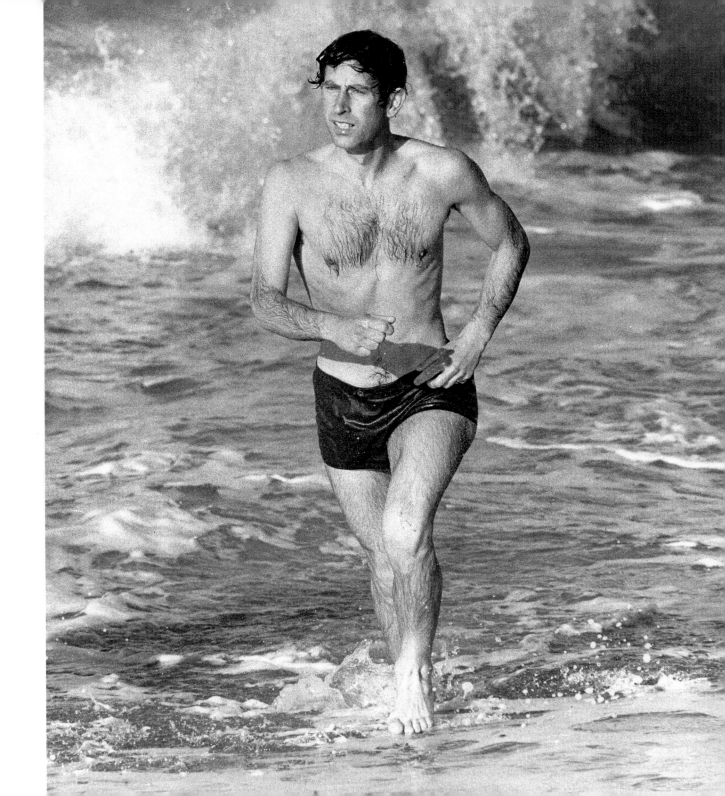

Tim Graham

Prince Edward at Cambridge University. This picture is one of a set taken to mark his 21st birthday.

Cambridge, England March 1985

Julian Calder

The Princess Royal returning from the State Opening of Parliament.

London November 1985

HRH The Duke of York

Balmoral Castle, left.

*Grampian, Scotland
11th September 1984*

Martin Cleaver

**Above, this was the only opportunity to photograph
Prince Andrew during the Falklands conflict and,
probably, the first anywhere of him holding a Nikon.**

Port Stanley, Falkland Islands June 1982

Tim Graham

The Prince of Wales, below,
sketching in the gardens of the
Imperial Palace.

Kyoto, Japan May 1986

Tim Graham

The Queen Mother, right, after
presenting the Irish Guards
with shamrocks on St Patrick's
Day joined them for a
regimental photograph.

West Germany, March 1984

Ian Wooldridge

Sports buffs like statistics so if you had to evolve a scoreline for the eighties I would say The Baddies beat The Goodies by 7-3. It is a subjective reckoning, of course, and may owe something to the fact that the sportswriter spends as much time back-stage as in the dress circle. Thus if I suggest that one of the most acclaimed performers of the decade was drugged up to the eyeballs and got away with it — while poor, dumb, bewildered, exploited Ben Johnson was transfixed into mumbling confession — you will get the drift.

It is obviously the eternal right of the paying customer to ignore the tainted and the tawdry. The honourable and the romantic still exist. You can still slumber in a deck-chair and watch, against the backdrop of Worcester Cathedral, a young man named Graeme Hick resurrect the golden age of batsmanship. You can still drive round that final curve into St Andrews, Scotland and immerse yourself in the religion of golf, the most impeccably mannered game in existence. You can still go to the great rugby parthenons of Twickenham, Murrayfield and Cardiff and there, though enveloped by the tunes of ardent nationalism, witness no quarter yielded in a battle without bullets. In the eighties we saw the America's Cup prised away from America's yachtsmen after a little matter of 132 years, and Sandy Lyle hit that impossible shot from sand in Augusta to win the US Masters Championship and Desert Orchid, the only human steeplechaser of our time, change down into third to come up that last cruel gradient at Cheltenham to win the Gold Cup by nothing less than divine right.

There was also, towards the end of the decade, a renaissance that no realist could have predicted. The Olympic monolith, shattered by political boycott in Moscow in 1980 and Los Angeles in 1984, rent by ideological schism, bent by commercialism, riddled with drugs, seemed doomed to die in Seoul, South Korea, in 1988. With enormous percipience I went there six months before they were due to start, observed the student rioting and the paranoic fear of a North Korean attack, and wrote precisely that. They proved to be the finest Games since Rome in 1960. All but five of the world's nations turned up and a proud Third World country, setting aside its internal differences, steadied a tottering Olympic movement and gave it new hope. Not even the protracted scandal of Ben Johnson's drug-fuelled run could ultimately tarnish South Korea's dignified triumph.

No, you wouldn't have wanted to be dead through the decade for it saw sport soar to new zeniths of heroic performance. But — and here, I am afraid, is where The Baddies come in after a slow start and pile up an insuperable lead — sport also simply reeled beneath the blows of cheating, commercial chicanery and sheer human catastrophe.

It was as though conscience no longer existed. 'Play on' said football after 39 people had been killed watching Liverpool in the Heysel Stadium, Brussels. And play on they did until 95 more who had arrived early to watch Liverpool take the field at Hillsborough, Sheffield, were crushed to death where they stood. Each time the police were blamed, as though they had gone in there with machine-guns and mown them down. It was incomprehensible but, disguising its callousness behind a brief display of black ties and a reassuring verse or two of 'You'll Never Walk Alone', football played on again, resisting and ridiculing those who attempted to impose practical crowd discipline.

Two other words coloured the decade. They were professionalism and commercialism, two extremely different animals.

There is nothing wrong with 'professionalism' in its true definition: the payment of money to the talented, be it at sport or driving furniture removal trucks.

Unfortunately the eighties saw the word corrupted into shadier interpretation. Adjectivally the 'professional' foul embraced slashing the legs beneath an opposing forward who had beaten you fair and square by skill and staying at the wicket when you knew you had been caught in the slips. 'Professionals' thus became the hard-men, the new red-badge-of-courage noun. It was also the synonym for cheat and of cheating there was plenty. The justification, of course, was that all the others are doing it and therefore one ought to join the club to survive. Therein lies the route to anarchy and sport took several long strides down that road.

Commercialism merely seduced it. To a degree that was more understandable but there were some desperately undignified scenes as the sincerely rich — the International Olympic Committee, Wimbledon, Manchester United Football Club — sincerely manoeuvred to get richer. The IOC sold its Winter Games to television, dragging out a once-compact programme into an interminable bore to get more money from more commercial advertisements. Wimbledon created a 'white market', its own self-created justification for re-selling returned debenture tickets at ten times their face value, as if that fooled anyone.

Manchester United, once of proud integrity, simply put itself up for sale to a number of dubious bidders like a fish-and-chip shop.

Commercialism had its even seamier side. Early on in the eighties, in Las Vegas, I watched sickened as an aging Muhammad Ali had that wonderfully alert brain smashed repeatedly into his skull in the terrible last three rounds of his fight with Larry Holmes. He had to fight on after that in an attempt to recover enough money to live. Where had forty million dollars disappeared? The vultures had won and Ali, by the end of the decade, was a shambling physical wreck. Boxing authorities called it Parkinson's Disease.

In the same town, late in the eighties, I watched Frank Bruno, of England, fight Mike Tyson, of the United States. Tyson was the greatest thing since Ali. In fact he was the greatest thing since sliced boxers: at just 22 he had already grossed more than thirty million dollars but in a court hearing involving a brief and disastrous marriage he openly admitted he had no idea where most of the money had gone.

You wept for Tyson. You wept for boxing. You wept for sport. I didn't weep for Frank Bruno that night because he fought bravely for himself, his family and Britain and, at the moment I write these words, has banked the £1 million he made in five courageous rounds without incurring terrible injury and shown no desperate anxiety to return to the prize ring. Pray God he never does. one million pounds, suitably invested, might just keep him in a manner to which he was never brought up.

But you see what sort of a decade it has been. Rich in achievement, desperate in disillusion, cruel, uplifting, brave, cowardly, deceitful, romantic, sickening. Sport in the eighties, I suppose, just about reflected what was happening elsewhere in the big wide world in which heroism came second to tyranny and terrorism.

David Ashdown

Keith Houchen scores for Coventry City against Tottenham Hotspur in the 1987 FA Cup Final.

Wembley Stadium, North London May 1987

Adrian Murrell

Mike Gatting is hit in the face by a Malcolm Marshall bouncer.

First one-day international, England v West Indies, Kingston, Jamaica January 1986

David Ashdown

Sebastian Coe at Crystal Palace.

South London 1985

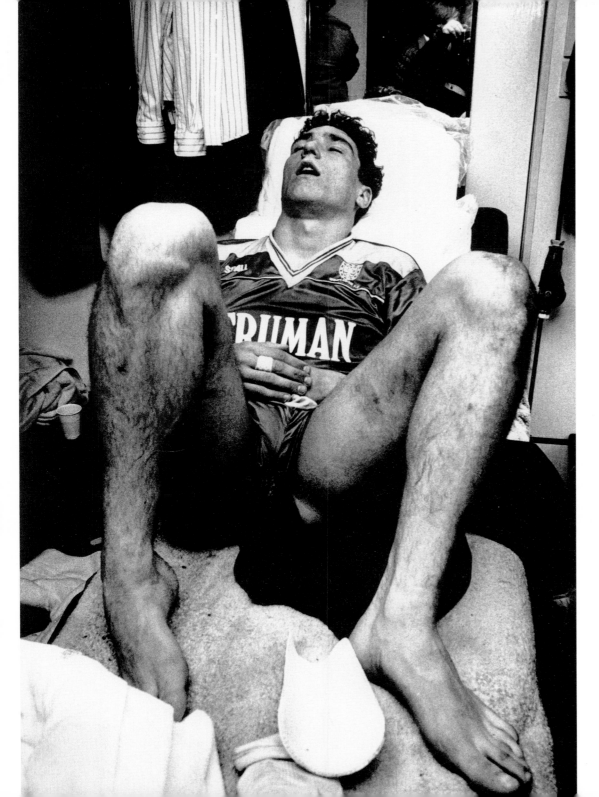

Herbie Knott

An exhausted Vinnie Jones sound asleep in the Plough Lane dressing room minutes after Wimbledon's epic 3-1 win over Everton in the 5th round of the FA Cup. Despite his ferocious reputation, off the field he is a gentle, friendly soul, happiest when shooting or fishing, having been brought up by his gamekeeper uncle in North Wales.

Wimbledon, South London
February 1987

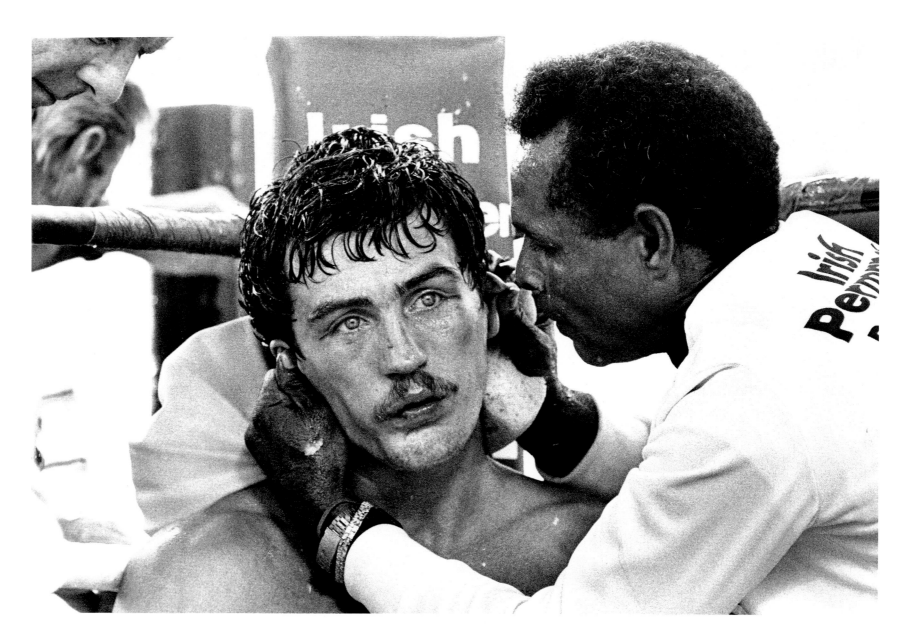

Chris Smith

Barry McGuigan.

Las Vegas, USA 1986

Eamonn McCabe

I followed Steve Davis into a press conference — and survived for two frames before I got kicked out.

Wembley Arena, North London 1982

Eamonn McCabe

A rare picture of Lester Piggott smiling, lit by some TV lights. He has always been a hero of mine, if one of the most awkward men I have nearly met.

Sandown, Surrey 1984

Adrian Murrell

Ian Botham.
Taken on the steps of the players'
area in the pavilion at St Vincent.
This picture was taken the day after
Botham and Gower went sailing
from St Vincent to Mustique whilst
England were losing their match to
the Windward Islands. This whole
tour was steeped in controversy
both on and off the field of play,
culminating in Botham sacking his
agent.

Windward Islands v England
West Indies January 1986

IN THE EVENT OF RAIN
SPECTATORS ARE REQUESTED
NOT TO RAISE UMBRELLAS
UNTIL PLAY HAS BEEN STOPPED

Steve Powell

**Torrential rain at
Wimbledon — a common
enough occurence — on this
occasion produced severe
flooding on the centre court.**

*Wimbledon
South London 1985*

Adrian Murrell

This was the first day/night one-day international match between England and West Indies in Sydney. Michael Holding bowling to Mike Brearley, then captain of England.

New South Wales, Australia
November 1979

Chris Smith

Opposite, greyhound racing.

Hackney, London 1986

Leo Mason

The best gig I ever had! Eight months in the winter sun of Australia on assignment for *Time* magazine, photographing the 1987 America's Cup. The 12m yacht shown here is the eventual winner, Stars & Stripes.

Fremantle, Western Australia December 1987

Steve Powell

Having smuggled my
scuba gear past the
security guards around
the Olympic pool,
opposite, I got this pre-
arranged shot of Tracey
Riuz and Candy Costee.
They won Olympic gold
just a couple of weeks
later.

Los Angeles, USA 1984

David Ashdown

Wayne Dobbins,
right, at the British
Short Course
Championships.

Ipswich, Suffolk 1986

Chris Smith

Seve Ballesteros, opposite, at the Open Championship.

Sandwich, Kent 1985

Patrick Eagar

English summer weather at Old Trafford. Test umpire Dickie Bird pulls up the stumps to allow the covers to be placed over the wicket.

Manchester, England 1985

Patrick Eagar

The ground floodlights came on gradually at the Sydney Cricket Ground just as the sun had set, lighting the horizon and providing a beautiful sky.

New South Wales, Australia
January 1983

Steve Powell

The Belgian solution to the World Cup skills of Diego Maradona.

Bernabeu Stadium, Madrid
Spain 1982

Leo Mason

This image epitomises the old adage about lucky pictures. The right lens, exposure and camera position, all combined to secure the exact moment that Daley Thompson's bid for a medal came to an ignominious end!

Olympic Games, Seoul, South Korea
September 1988

Bob Martin

Wendy Williams. I shot this at dawn so that the light would only reflect on the diver and not on the pool.

Mission Bay, Florida, USA 1988

John Kobal

Is there a star more radiant than the Princess of Wales? Or more charismatic than Mikhail Gorbachev? Or fiercer than Mike Tyson? Or any more famous?

In theory, all celebrities are assumed to be camera-friendly. In practice, only a very few are beyond the moment of notoriety.

News shots of celebrities are predicated on the premise that the reader knows who they are and wants to see them. This has nothing to do with whether or not they are camera-friendly — a statesman from some tinpot republic, driving to see the Queen, gets his picture in the paper. Sometimes someone in the crowd has one of those faces about which you want to know more. Nine times out of ten it turns out they have the type of personality to match. This personality is a rich tapestry. Stars without personalities would be like the Queen without her crown. Or an astronaut without his ship. As long as a star can retain that quality made up of their wonder and our curiosity they remain stars.

All movie stars are celebrities. All celebrities are not movie stars. Think of the celebrated models who try to project their catwalk personalities before the camera, only to discover their appeal is tied to a clothes rack.

The camera to the movie star is what an instrument is to the soloist. The camera will record the singer singing, dancer dancing, actor acting. But it will love the movie star. They are that unique breed of celebrity who are, or have been, camera-friendly. Their existence, a by-product of the camera and inconceivable without it — is the pre-eminent form of celebrity in our century.

Sophia Loren, in town to promote a book on beauty, is no longer the twenty-year-old peasant girl exuding sensuality and lit from a thousand different directions to show her in the best possible light — that was what made her — now she is 'off-set'. A mature, still beautiful woman who is marketing. But she has been famous for so long now, that she can afford to be ordinary, to appear to do nothing except what pleases her. She doesn't worry that her career might suffer because of unflattering pictures. She doesn't even retreat into the flashing, cheesy smile that lifts a chin. Her thoughts seem to be elsewhere than the moment, and the gesture of a woman preening herself in front of the mirror, as beautiful women have done in countless paintings and photographs, seems as much part of her daily routine as the warm-up is to the dancer. Nothing is given away. But Loren has become a legend, and thus forever camera-friendly.

When a subject is not instantly recognisable by name their face should still give their game away. The effectiveness of a photo of a celebrity is that the public responds to it as if they recognise who it is — as when an unknown Hedy Lamarr strolled through the casbah of Algiers, her first American film, and became a star with one close-up. You didn't know the face but you knew she had to be a movie star. And it's not the trappings. It's in the relationship between the naked face and the camera's naked eye. It's ironic that one of the most camera-friendly faces of this century, Garbo, shied away from the camera to such an extent that her name went on to become synonymous with elusiveness.

A news photographer needs a shot to please his editor, and at most has a few minutes with a lot of other photographers crowding around to get a picture good enough for his next edition. Even if the star is co-operative, news photographers are looking for an angle. With women the classic is cleavage, but the 'big' stars reserve that for the big screen. Men are more difficult to make exciting. Not every man is a natural like Peter Ustinov. In any case, the news photographer is not glamourising or enlarging the public's perception of the celebrity. They are there because of what the star has achieved, not to help them achieve it. They've done their job by getting to the star. It's up to the star to make sure they come out well under flash-fire.

To a star, unlike the average person, being photographed is like an interview for which they don't have to make up lines, only to cover those they have. In some eighty years of movies, and movie stars, a mere handful have had the ability to illuminate pictures taken of them that were not specially posed or lit in advance: Crawford, Bogart and Marilyn Monroe come to mind. They looked what they were in pictures taken of them, whether sick in bed, in tears leaving a courtroom, lonely and dejected on a beach, with a drink in a bar at the end of a long night and naturally, inevitably, surrounded by the adulation of their admirers. In the crush of a premiere these people towered. They glow in the vicinity of a camera. The lens was a second skin to them; the aperture — their pores; the shutter — their pulse. There couldn't be an unflattering angle of them because they were intuitively in harmony with the camera.

But despite the millions of images created worldwide over the past eighty years and of the thousands of people who made it, for a time, enduring examples are rare.

In short, a celebrities must project to protect themselves from a bad photograph. Ego must not be allowed to show. Boredom tends to produce more unflattering photos than obesity. Impatience plays straight into the photographer's lens. A suggestion of self-importance spells death e.g.

Barbra Streisand. 'Film' celebrities, unlike almost any other kind for whose talents the public is willing to spend money, owe as much of their success to what the public sees in them as to their own effort to achieve this pinnacle of adulation. Even today, with sport and rock, TV and video all vying for media attention (as distinct from merely being a media celebrity), what celebrities — short of our own Royals — are more compelling or 'starry' than the movie star? To say that movie stars have a duty to their public always to look their best, is not to say that they need always be dressed to the nines and made up to the gills, but that their picture will convey as much of their essential quality as a star as on screen.

Robert Redford, Michele Pfeiffer, Tom Cruise or Dustin Hoffman, be he ever so humble, are camera-friendly. Unlike the starlet on the beach in Cannes, polluting herself in the Med to get her picture in the papers, they have to sell nothing for the photographers to be in pursuit.

During the production of a documentary about Marlene Dietrich, for which the legendary star was to be heard in conversation but never seen, director Maxamilian Schell could be heard pleading with her to let him film her. The then 86-year-old actress steadfastly rejected all his reasons, concluding the discussion with 'I have been photographed to death'.

Herbie Knott

Peter Ustinov on location. Here he was as natural as you're ever likely to see him. A likeable man.

England March 1985

Nobby Clark

Sir Ralph Richardson on his 79th birthday at home.

London 1981

Jill Furmanovsky

John Hurt, taken for *Time Out* magazine. They commissioned a cover and this was one of the out-takes. It was around the time that the film *Scandal* was released.

South Bank, London 11th January 1989

Jill Furmanovsky

Terence Stamp taken for *Time Out* magazine. He was in conversation with John McVicar in the gardens of the Chelsea Arts Club.

London 9th August 1984

Nobby Clark

Billy Connolly in his dressing room at the Albany Theatre.

Deptford, South London 1985

Nobby Clark

Sophia Loren in her hotel bedroom at Claridges.

London 1980

Nobby Clark

Barry Humphries in his dressing room at the Piccadilly Theatre.

London 1980

Nobby Clark

Dave Allen backstage at the Fairfield Halls.

Croydon, Surrey 1983

Suresh Karadia

Left, Ben Elton, photographed
at his home in Islington.

North London 1989

Mike Maloney

Ernie Wise, opposite, pictured at
his home on the day that his
partner Eric Morecambe died. I
rang Ernie at home to ask if he
would see me and took this
picture in front of one of his
favourite photographs of the two
of them.

Bray, Middlesex 28th May 1984

Richard Mildenhall

Above, Opera North's production of 'Carmen'. Opposite, Georgian State Dance Company.

Grand Theatre, Leeds 12th December 1987 and Palladium Theatre, London 18th May 1987

Richard Mildenhall

Brian Glover plays God.
This picture was taken from the
lighting rig area so as to incorporate
the strange lighting props.

Bill Bryden's Mystery Plays Trilogy
Cottesloe Theatre, London
15th January 1985

Jill Furmanovsky

Dennis Potter.
An hour in his company was a privilege.

London 2nd October 1986

Allan Titmuss

It's not widely known, but photographers usually get just the first few songs at a concert. Three is normal, though James Brown and Prince have recently decreed one, Michael Jackson and Robert Palmer two.

For Madonna at Wembley Stadium there was another snag. The stage was roughly where the goal posts normally stand.

Photographers would have to work from the half-way line commentary boxes, half a football pitch away, and for just the first three numbers. With a 600mm Nikkor, Madonna from head to toe occupied less than a third of the frame.

Seventy thousand people in Wembley Stadium were there to see her. She turns her back and dances away. The music was dull. The manipulation shining. Even the record company people were bored and embarrassed. Once in a while it's a relief being kicked out after three numbers.

Wembley Stadium,
North London
18th August 1987

Dave Hogan

Michael Jackson at the start of his world tour. On the first night of the Tokyo concerts, I was given permission to photograph the concert from the very back of the baseball stadium. After threatening to commit hara-kiri the authorities allowed me into the pit for concert number two where I shot this picture.

Tokyo, Japan 1st September 1987

Jill Furmanovsky

Ivy and Lux, below.
This was taken in Ivy
and Lux's bedroom while
the band 'The Cramps'
were on tour. They are
singer and bass player
respectively and the
band (and the couple)
are still going strong
now.

Edinburgh
Lothian, Scotland
May 1981

Dave Hogan

Forewarned of a surprise
appearance by David
Bowie I made my way to
the front of the stage and
offered to send prints to
the frantic fans to make
them settle down for long
enough to get this shot.

NEC Birmingham
1987

Dave Hogan

The picture was taken after a press conference. As Mick Jagger left the conference one of the photographers said something 'smart' to Mick, hence the startled expression.

London 1984

Herbie Knott

Walter Weller, opposite, conducting the Royal Liverpool Philharmonic Orchestra in rehearsal for a gala performance featuring six of the orchestra's conductors from 1963 onwards. Weller was principal conductor and artistic advisor from 1977 to 1980.

Liverpool
29th August 1987

Allan Titmuss

Miles Davis. Looking through some of my pictures in July 1989, mostly those of his old collaborator Gil Evans, Miles Davis said, 'I don't look at pictures of myself any more — every time I do, another piece has dropped off.' Then he found this. 'Ah, this one', he said, 'I've seen this one lots. I like this one.'

Royal Festival Hall
London 20th July 1985

Allan Titmuss

Three changes of costume in as many numbers. Prince, left, the ironist chameleon, suddenly lifted his sweater in the midst of a song. Over in a blink, I don't think anyone else caught it.

Wembley Arena,
North London
13th August 1986

Suresh Karadia

Grace Jones the singer, opposite, during her visit to Madame Tussaud's when she sat for the sculptor. Her wax likeness was on display.

London 26th February 1987

Simon Hoggart

Politicians have a problem with pictures, for each has to serve two purposes. They must depict the politician as a wise, contemplative statesman, and at the same time reveal him or her as essentially a human being like the rest of us, which of course most of them are not, or else they wouldn't be politicians. The Americans find this fact easier to cope with than Europeans. The principal role of the US president is, these days, to be the nation's Best Friend. George Bush is forever being snapped doing 'guy' things, such as fishing, tossing horseshoes, or working up a good, glossy expensive sweat while jogging in the company of approximately eight hundred Secret Service agents. In 1985 Ronald Reagan left hospital after having had a cancerous tumour removed and made a little speech thanking the staff while wearing a baseball hat. This was meant to depict him as a regular fellow. It's quite unimagineable that, say, François Mitterrand would appear at a similar occasion wearing the French equivalent, a jaunty beret.

Mrs Thatcher, for all her concern about being seen as a 'conviction' politician, has paid closer attention to her image than any recent prime minister (though Harold Wilson was careful too; he was never photographed with his favourite means of relaxation, a cigar and a glass of brandy — this would have damaged the picture of an ordinary working man who happened to smoke a pipe the size of Drax B).

Sir Gordon Reece, the former ad man and TV producer, who first persuaded Mrs Thatcher to soften her voice, also got rid of the fussy necklines and strings of pearls which she had favoured until then.

He had her hair made softer and less like a bouffant helmet. Yet every strand always remains in place. It was he who had her pictured at the sink, washing up, as part of her campaign for the Tory leadership. It was not a particularly convincing image, though she was greatly helped when her rival, Willie Whitelaw, decided to follow her example. He looked as if he was saying 'So I just put the plate in the soapy water and dab, do I?' Even when she is at her ease, Thatcher's photographs always depict the Mother of her People, vigilant through the days and nights on their behalf, or at least what she imagines is their behalf.

Often public figures use the camera to lie for themselves. Denis Healey, a tough, brutal political operator who is also highly educated, wanted to be seen a jovial card, your favourite uncle doing his Les Dawson impression again. For years the papers were full of pictures showing Denis mugging at the camera, like a middle-aged yob on holiday in Spain. Norman Tebbit, in real life quite an amiable soul, wanted to be thought of as a monster, a terrifying political enemy. Pictures are rare which do not show Tebbit scowling. Film is used for a complicated double bluff.

A huge recent bonus for politicians has been the improvement in the standards of newspaper reproduction. When I joined the northern office of *The Guardian* two decades ago, the paper employed some of the best staff photographers in the country. Yet it was printed on what looked like fish wrapping — indeed, in those days, fish wrapping is just what it was. These highly skilled men would be close to tears as a particularly choice picture, the result of hours of work, would appear like a box Brownie snap printed on an Indian *dhurrie*.

The remarkable improvement has allowed papers to print real portraits, a medium which politicians adore. (I once watched the late Marc Boxer darting around a cabinet minister, making sketches for a cartoon. Every time Boxer moved, the politician had to switch the angle of his jaw in a frantic effort to look statesmanlike from every perspective. Photographic portraits must be worse.)

As a result we have seen the rise of the fake informal picture, most often employed on the eve of the Budget. Chancellors like to invite the Sunday press up to their country homes where they can be snapped in an Aran sweater, walking the dog in the direction of the local pub. Or else surrounded by their children, if photogenic enough, generally looking as if Daddy was in the middle of reading them a heart-warming story. The pictures look as relaxed and informal as a Japanese funeral.

Politicians, like union leaders and editors, are fortunate in that, on the whole, people aren't terribly interested in them. The paparazzi don't hang around restaurants and night clubs because John Major — or even Andrew Neil or Peregrine Worsthorne — have been spotted there. Occasionally someone will be unlucky, like David Steel here, beset by Cleo Rocos, or Jeremy Thorpe, facing trial on murder charges. But there are no recorded instances of John Smith MP lashing out at an intrusive snapper, or Norman Fowler getting into a fight with any lensman. Usually politicians only need to worry about the unexpected pratfall, as when Neil Kinnock was knocked over by a wave on Brighton beach at the conference where he became Labour Party leader, or the unguarded expression, simultaneously frozen and exaggerated in the blinding moment of the flash.

Alan Grisbrook

A close encounter for David Steel and Cleo Rocos.

London 1987

Ed Pritchard

Shot in 1986 as part of a continuing personal project.

Westminster, London 1986

John Sturrock

Edward Heath pictured at the Conservative party conference.

Blackpool, Lancashire 1987

Adrian Murrell

Mrs Ghandi's funeral. Photographers often get pigeon-holed as specialising in certain subjects so for me it was a refreshing experience working with top news photographers and approaching a job which had a different viewpoint from that of sport.

New Delhi, India 4th November 1984

Herbie Knott

We had some differences about where to shoot the picture. Lawson's PR man suggested a gloomy, bare room in No. 11. No thanks. We tried his study, but that was so dismally tidy, that when I walked in and found Lawson sitting bolt upright behind his desk saying, 'I expect you want me like this', my answer was, again no thanks. Some humming and ha-ing followed, before we settled for the garden. Several minions had to be dispatched to unravel the various security systems barring our way. Not, perhaps, his natural habitat.

Downing Street, London September 1987

John Sturrock

Michael Heseltine gives a press conference after his resignation from the Cabinet.

London 1986

Suresh Karadia

Theology of liberation: Anthony Wedgwood Benn, left, Labour MP for Bristol South-East.

St James's Church, Piccadilly, London 3rd March 1983

John Sturrock

Neil and Glenys Kinnock, opposite, on the campaign trail leading up to the general election.

South Wales 1987

Sally Fear

Brenda Dean, leader of Britain's biggest print union, SOGAT, at the time of the strike against News International.

London March 1986

Mike Maloney

David Steel MP had just been voted the winner of a competition called 'Head of the Year' sponsored by the Hairdressing Federation of Great Britain. The presentation to the winner always takes place at the Waldorf Hotel, London. After 30 minutes of explaining to David why it would be good publicity for him to pose with this wig, he agreed. The picture made every paper the next day. In my paper — the *Daily Mirror* — we used it on page one.

London
20th February 1984

Suresh Karadia

Ken Livingstone, opposite. At the time he
was leader of the Greater London Council.

Westminster, London 14th February 1983

Mike Abrahams

Norman Tebbit at the Conservative party conference.

Bournemouth, Dorset October 1986

Herbie Knott

A week before the 1983 general election. At 12.45 am Margaret Thatcher finishes an evening of speech writing by going through her constituency mail. She was up at 6 am the same morning.

Downing Street, London June 1983